Are We Having Fun Yet?

by Bill Griffith

Zippy the Pinhead's

29 Day Guide To Random Activities and Arbitrary Donuts

E.P. DUTTON • NEW YORK

Book design and production: Bill Griffith
Typography: Ampersand Design and typo/graphics
Negatives and camera work: G. Howard, Inc.

Published in the United States by E.P. Dutton,
a division of New American Library
2 Park Avenue, New York, N.Y. 10016

Library of Congress Catalog Card Number 85-072160

ISBN: 0-525-48184-2

Published simultaneously in Canada by Fitzhenry & Whiteside
Limited, Toronto

10 9 8 7 6 5 4 3 2 1

First Edition

W

Thanks to: Paul Yamamoto, Paul DeAngelis,
Joel Goldstein and Patty Graves.

DEDICATION

To *Diane Noomin,* whose help with
this book was invaluable and is all
the more appreciated considering
the fact that she rarely speaks in
non-sequiturs.

ITINERARY

"There's nothing like eating under
an open sky, even if it is radioactive."

Frankie Avalon in
"Panic in the Year Zero" (1962)

FUN: THE CONCEPT

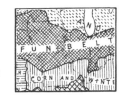

I'M **ZIPPY** THE **PIN-HEAD** AND I'M TOTALLY COMMITTED TO THE FESTIVE MODE.

I'M IN **DIRECT** DAILY CONTACT WITH MANY ADVANCED FUN **CONCEPTS..**

I KNOW THINGS ABOUT **TROY DONAHUE** THAT CAN'T EVEN BE **PRINTED !!**

TROY AND I ARE LIKE **THIS--**

ONCE, THERE WAS **NO** FUN... The **PRE-FUN VOID**

BUT WHAT **IS** FUN? WHY IS IT USUALLY **DAY-GLO PINK**? AND **WHERE** DOES IT GO WHEN **EDWIN MEESE** COMES OVER?

THIS WAS BEFORE **MENU** PLANNING, **FASHION** STATEMENTS OR **NAUT-ILUS** EQUIPMENT...

THEN, IN **1985..**

FUN WAS COMPLETE-LY ENCODED ON THIS TINY **MICROCHIP..** IT CONTAINS 14,768 VAGUELY AMUS-ING **SIT-COM** PILOTS!

WE HAD TO WAIT **FOUR BILLION** YEARS BUT WE FINALLY GOT **JERRY LEWIS**, **MTV** & A LARGE SELECTION OF **CREME-FILLED SNACK CAKES!**

HOWEVER, IN THE NEXT **29** DAYS, YOU CAN ENJOY AN **ADULT** RE-LATIONSHIP WITH **427** ADDITIONAL FUN FACTS WITHOUT EVER LEAVING THE PRIVACY OF YOUR UNWANTED **CONDO!**

YOU MAY WITNESS ARGUMENTS BETWEEN **LARGE WOMEN** & CHILDREN IN **CHEAP** JOGGING SUITS.

FROZEN ENTREÉS MAY BE FLUNG BY MEMBERS OF OPPOSING **SWANSON SECTS..**

AND THREE **PSYCHICS** ON A FOUR DAY CRIME SPREE WILL FIND A CURE FOR **NUDISM.**

SHELF-LIFE EXPLAINS TO ZIPPY THAT **OBJECTIVE REALITY** DEMANDS A **RATIONAL RESPONSE**..

ZIPPY EXPLAINS TO SHELF-LIFE THAT IT'S **HIS** TURN TO **WALK** THE **WHIRL-O-MATIC**...

AS SHELF-LIFE HEADS FOR THE **LAUNDRY ROOM,** ZIPPY REFLECTS ON THE JOYS OF **FUN OWNERSHIP**...

SOMETIMES YOU HAVE TO GET **TOUGH** WITH FUN...

..OR IT'LL JUST **TAKE** ALL YOU'VE GOT TO **GIVE** AND ASK FOR **MORE**..

DON'T TRY TO STOP ME...

FRIVOLITY IS A STERN **TASKMASTER**...

Ⓜ EANWHILE, UNTIL THE BOTTOM DROPS OUT OF **PORK FUTURES,** ZIPPY INSISTS ON PUTTING THE **FUNMOBILE** INTO HIGH GEAR AND CRUISING DOWN THE **FREEWAY** OF **FUN** AS WE KNOW IT--

I **KNOW** WHAT YOU'RE THINKING..

WHY ARE THOSE **3 CUBISTS** TAILING ME AND ARE THEY **STILL** ON A 4-DAY **EGG HUNT?**

9

ZIPPY'S *RIGHT*..THREE CUBISTS ARE INDEED CLOSING IN...

..THEY'RE *DETERMINED* TO GIVE HIM A *PURPOSE* IN LIFE..

..AHEAD OF THEM LAY A VAST, *UNCHARTED* NEIGHBORHOOD...

FOLLOW THAT *IMPULSE!!*

THEY WERE *YOUNG*, THEY WERE *RESTLESS*, THEY'D 'SEEN TOO MANY RE-RUNS OF "*STARSKY* AND *HUTCH*"...

I CAN'T DECIDE WHICH *WRONG TURN* TO MAKE FIRST!! I WONDER IF *BOB GUCCIONE* HAS THESE PROBLEMS!

YOW!! UP AHEAD! IT'S *DONUT HUT!!*

RANDOM ACTIVITIES 1

MENU PLANNING

ENJOY THESE VISUALLY STIM- ULATING *MEALTIME* HINTS REGARDLESS OF RACE OR TIME ZONE..

..YOU'LL NEED A *DINING* UTENSIL!!

BRUNCHTIME PANCAKES WITH *LAMB CHUNKS* IN A SPRIGHTLY SAUCE OF BLENDED *KIWIS* & *GATORADE.*

LUNCHTIME FROOT LOOPS AND *MAYO* WITH *LICORICE WHIPS* ON A *7-GRAIN BUN!!*

ANYTIME A FRESH ROULADE OF *WON-TON* WRAPPERS & WINTER- GREEN MINTS WITH A *FROSTY* MUG OF *LIME* & *CLAM* JUICE...

Court Returns Brain to Owner

In Pittsburgh, Pa., **Judge Robert E. Dauer** ruled yester- day that the human brain confis- cated by police from **John Hri- cak** on August 7 should right- fully be returned to him.

Police had been in the pro- cess of raiding Hricak's home for drugs when they seized the brain, which had been preserved in formaldehyde, in a jar on a coffee table.

Assistant District Attorney Daniel Fitzsimmons argued that Hricak, who called the brain "George," was "denigrating the value of human life."
—News Story

DID YOU TELL THEM ANY- THING?

NAH..

YOU THINK I'M OUTTA MY SKULL?

DETOUR 2
THE HUMAN BRAIN

CUBISM WAS ONLY A CLEVER *FRONT* FOR THESE THREE CAGEY *CAREER* COUNSELORS..

THEY HAD PLANS, THEY GAVE SEMINARS &, ON THE SIDE, THEY SOLD *INSURANCE*..

"HELLO, BRIAN..."

VERNON LAZNOFF CARRIED HIS **BRAINS** IN A JAR. HE SAID THEY RECEIVED MESS-AGES FROM **JULIO IGLESIAS** & THE **PENTAGON.** SINCE ZIPPY **ALSO** RE-CEIVED MESSAGES FROM **JULIO IGLESIAS** AND THE **PENTAGON,** THE TWO BECAME INSTANT TENNIS PARTNERS...

"KNOW OF ANY GOOD **PARTIES**?"

SEVERAL CORPORATE **ATTORNEYS** ON A NOON RECESS JOINED **ZIPPY** AT THE COUNTER --

"IT'S ALL **CLEARED UP** NOW.."

"WHAT'S THAT? TODAY'S **SPECIAL**?"

"I ONCE HAD A LARGE **NOON RECESS**.."

FOR A MOMENT, ZIPPY WAS **CONFUSED**.. A MOMENT **LATER** HE WAS **FLUSTERED**... THIS WAS FOLLOWED BY 3 MOMENTS OF **DISARRAY**..

"I'LL BE BRIEF.."

POP!

THEN HE UNEXPECTEDLY BEGAN RECEIVING **MESSAGES** FROM **VERNON LAZNOFF**..

THE HUMAN BRAIN, ZIPPY ASSERTED, WAS DIVIDED INTO **NORTHERN ITALY** & **SOUTHERN ITALY**..

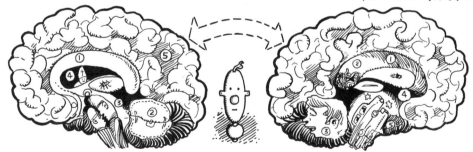

IN THE **NORTH** WE FIND THOUGHTS OF **MODULAR FURNITURE**① SIDE BY SIDE WITH A **LEATHER HANDBAG**② AND TWO **INDUSTRIALISTS**③ IN DARK GLASSES DISCUSSING TRADE DEFICITS WITH THE **POPE**④. PURELY **ANALYTICAL FUNCTIONS**, SUCH AS **ORDERING** A PLATE OF **GNOCCHI**⑤, ARE LO-CATED IN THIS HALF OF THE BRAIN.

IN THE **SOUTH** WE STUMBLE ACROSS THE ENTRANCE TO A MYSTERIOUS **CATA-COMB**①, LITTERED WITH DUBBED **SPAGH-ETTI WESTERNS**② & AN ANGUISHED CRY FROM **MARCELLO MASTROIANNI**③. IN THE "**FISSURE OF ROLANDO**"④ ALL PURELY **INTUITIVE** FUNCTIONS, SUCH AS **CONSUMING** A PLATE OF GNOCCHI, ARE FOUND DODGING KAMIKAZE **TAXI CABS**.⑤

NEXT, LET'S HIKE UP THE **MEDULLA OBLONGATA!**

HERE I AM IN THE **POSTERIOR OLFACTORY LOBULE** BUT I DON'T SEE **CARL SAGAN** ANYWHERE!!

Ding Dongs

UNCONTROLLABLE URGE 500 FT.

OUTTA MY WAY, **McJERK!!**

Mc PUFF, Mc PANT..

WAIT! AREN'T YOU A **REVERED** CHILDHOOD MEMORY?

JESUS McCHRIST!

WHTTTT

DEEP IN THE HEART OF THE **ANTERIOR FORNIX** ZIPPY CAME UPON THE **ID**, THAT PART OF CONSCIOUSNESS WHICH RESPONDS POSITIVELY TO **HALF-OFF SALES**, SIX-PACKS OF **PAULI GIRL** AND **RONALD REAGAN'S** MEDIA PERSONALITY--

YOW!! I JUST **OUTLAWED** RUSSIA!

WHAT ABOUT TH' FUTURE OF THE **HUMAN RACE?**

HUH?

OR FLOSSING AFTER SNACKS?

I LIVE FOR THE **McMOMENT**, PAL!!

SO IF WE'RE NOT GONNA HAVE CASUAL **SEX** OR LISTEN TO **VAN HALEN** 'TIL WE DROP, I'M McOUTTA HERE!

Mc CIAO!!

GRRR...

..NUCLEAR HOLOCAUST.... ..ENVIRONMENTAL DISASTER..

..ECONOMIC COLLAPSE... ...RACISM.... ..& SCIENTOLOGY.

15

RANDOM ACTIVITIES 2

DATING
THE OPPOSITE SEX

THINGS WILL GO A LOT BETTER FOR YOU ONCE YOU REALIZE THAT *MATE SELECTION* IS DETERMINED BY *ALIEN COMPUTERS* FROM *ARCTURUS 14.*

PRIMPING IF THERE'S ONE *THING* THE OPPOSITE SEX DIS-LIKES IT'S STRAY *POPPY SEEDS.*

PREENING USE A DURABLE, ALL-WEATHER *WAX* ON YOUR-SELF *AND* YOUR *'66 BUICK!*

PASSING OUT CHOOSE A POPULAR SUBURBAN *BOWLING ALLEY*...WAIT UNTIL CLOSING TIME. THIS ONE'S *SURE FIRE!!*

ONLY A DREAM

BEYOND A SHALLOW LAKE, FIVE TINY FIGURES GATHERED AT THE GREEN OF THE 18TH HOLE. ZIPPY WANTED TO PLAY VERY BADLY, DESPITE AN EXTREMELY HIGH HANDICAP.

HE FLOATED ACROSS THE LAKE AND HOVERED ABOVE THE GOLFERS.

17

A HEATED ARGUMENT WAS IN PROGRESS. THE NUDE MODEL ACCUSED THE LAWMAN OF IMPOTENCE AND A FAILURE TO APPRECIATE KIERKEGAARD'S ABNEGATION THEORY. THE COP BROUGHT UP HER PILL DEPENDENCY AND OBVIOUS NEO-HEGELIAN PRECONCEPTIONS.

WHEN THE DISCUSSION TURNED TO INCLUDE THE CUBIST'S DUBIOUS GENETIC MAKE-UP, ZIPPY SUNK A 43 FOOT PUTT FROM A DIFFICULT LIE. THIS UNEXPECTED MARCH OF EVENTS GAVE ZIPPY A BOGIE BUT PROMPTED AN EMOTIONAL DISPLAY FROM THE GRIM REAPER.

HE PICKED UP A NUMBER ONE WOOD & BLASTED ZIPPY 190 YARDS DOWN THE FAIRWAY.
ZIPPY HAD A VISION OF LOIS LANE LOCKED IN A LUSTY EMBRACE WITH YOSEMITE SAM.
NEXT THING HE KNEW, ZIPPY WAS LOCKED IN A LUSTY EMBRACE WITH YOSEMITE SAM.

For the most trivial event to become an adventure, all you have to do is start telling about it. This is what deceives people: a man is always a teller of stories: he lives surrounded by his stories. He tries to live his life as if it were a story he was telling.

But you have to choose: live or tell. While you live, nothing happens. The scenery changes, people come in and go out, that's all. There are no beginnings. Days add on to days without rhyme or reason. I wanted the moments of my life to follow each other and order themselves as well as try to catch time by the tail.

OH YEH? MY **BIOLOGICAL ALARM CLOCK** JUST WENT OFF.. IT HAS A NOISELESS **DOZE FUNCTION** & FULL KITCHEN !!

THAT WAS WHEN THE CADDY APPEARED. JEAN-PAUL HAD BEEN KEEPING SCORE BEHIND A BUST OF
MAMIE VAN DOREN. ZIPPY LISTENED AS THE PHILOSOPHIZING BALL-CHASER CROONED
IN A HIGH-PITCHED MONOTONE. HE COULDN'T FOLLOW THE BEAT BUT HE LIKED THE LYRICS.

THE TWO THINKERS STROLLED ACROSS THE HIMALAYAS BY WAY OF IDAHO, TOOK A LEFT AT NORTH KOREA AND CAME OUT OF THE COLD FOR A COUPLE OF HOT PERNODS IN A LITTLE BISTRO ZIPPY KNEW PERSONALLY ON THE RUE DE CUISINART.

"WHY DO I HAVE THE FEELING THIS DREAM IS COSTING ME $55 AN HOUR?", ZIPPY THOUGHT TO HIMSELF & ANYONE ELSE WHO WOULD LISTEN. WHAT HE HAD WAS AN EXISTENTIAL CADDY AND A MORAL CRISIS. WHAT HE NEEDED WAS AN ORDER OF ROAST PORK APPETIZER.

RANDOM ACTIVITIES 3

DRESSING FOR ELLIOT NESS

ELLIOT NESS IS AN IMPECCABLE DRESSER AND **INSISTS** ALL THOSE AROUND HIM WEAR **TIGHT** 3-PIECE SUITS MADE OF A THICK, **SCRATCHY** WOOL.

BE STIFF NEVER SHOW ANY SIGN OF **HUMAN EMOTION**. DON'T BEND AT THE WAIST OR INDULGE IN **SYNCHRONIZED SWIMMING**.

BE FORMAL ALL **WOMEN** ARE TO BE ADDRESSED AS "**MA'AM**" AND TAKEN IN FOR QUESTIONING. **MEN** ARE TO BE ADDRESSED AS "**YOU BUM**".

BE ROBERT STACK THINK OF **WOOD**, **GRANITE** OR NORWAY'S LARGEST GLACIAL FORMATIONS. DECLINE ALL TALK SHOW INVITATIONS.

ADOPT MY LIFESTYLE OR I'LL HAVE TO PRESS CHARGES.

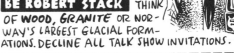

OK, YOUR **ID'S** ADJUSTED.. HERE'S MY **BILL**!

ONE MORE **PICK-UP** AN' I CALL IT A DAY..

AH, BUT I **AM** THE BILL.. ..THE BILL **IN** ITSELF AND **OF** ITSELF.. TRANS-CENDING TOWARD--

SHRINKS 'n STUFF MEDICAL BUILDING

FAST FUNERAL 'n ROOFING

CLAUDE **FUNSTON** MAKES PICK-UPS & DELIVERIES FOR **INTERSPURT EXPRESS** -

HE LIVES IN A **MOBILE HOME** & KNOWS NOTHING ABOUT CUBISM..

I HOPE MY **TEAM** WINS TODAY!!

PUSH

DON'T MIND **ME**, SIR..I'LL JUST GRAB THIS PAR-CEL EAR-MARKED FOR **DETROIT**!

EAR-MARKED?

..TO..

WELL, I'LL BE GOIN'.. HAVE A **NICE** DAY!

"**ONE** SIZE FITS **ALL**.."

HEY, **PAL**, SOMETHIN' I CAN DO FOR YOU? I'M PRETTY **BUSY**...

I HAVE TO TALK TO YOU ABOUT THE **UNITED STATES**..

ZIPPY BECAME HELPLESSLY **FIXATED** ON THE **SNAP-TAB** AT THE BACK OF CLAUDE'S ACRYLIC **HAT**. IT SPOKE OF **MANY THINGS**.. HE FOLLOWED IT TO THE PARKING LOT...

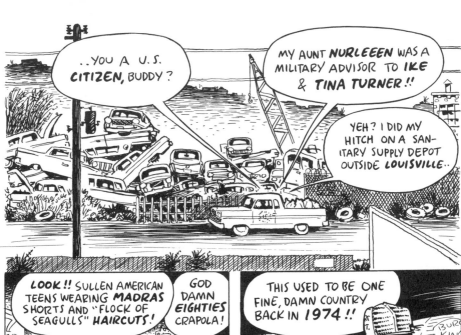

23

I HATE TH' EIGHTIES...

WOMEN WITH THEIR HAIR **CHOPPED OFF** AT TH' SIDE & WEARIN' GODDAM BAGGED-OUT **TWEED OVERCOATS!**

DID YOU KNOW **ZOMBIES** RULE **BELGIUM?**

C'MON, **GALS!** LET'S GET INTO **MYLAR** HIP-HUGGERS!!

HEY.

IMPORTED!!

HE **EARLY SEVENTIES** WAS THE **GOLDEN AGE** OF FEMALE ALLURE... THESE FASHIONS WILL MAKE A **BIG** COMEBACK SOMETIME BEFORE **1997!!**

YUP.. THERE'S A **BIG HOLE** INSIDE ME WHERE **LATEX HOT PANTS** USED T'BE---

GRASS SHACK DRIVE IN SINCE 1947

I GUESS THE ONLY THING TO DO ABOUT IT IS TO GET **LAID, LOADED** & LEFT FOR **DEAD**...

I'M FEELING **SPIRITUAL,** TOO, CLAUDE..

GRASS SHACK

ZIPPY AND CLAUDE SIPPED *BEERS* FOR 2 HOURS AND GOT MORE & MORE *PHILOSOPHICAL*...

RANDOM ACTIVITIES 4

HOW TO LAUGH

WHEN YOU HEAR A *JOKE* TOLD BY A *PROFESSIONAL* COMIC, YOU NEED THESE *CUES* TO AID YOU IN THE *HUMORISTIC* PROCESS..

I'LL LAUGH AT *ANYTHING* AS LONG AS IT'S OF *U.S.* ORIGIN!

ABSORB WATCH FOR SYMPATHETIC *BODY* LANGUAGE & GOOD GROOMING. LISTEN FOR *NEW YORK* ACCENT. (KNOW YOUR *YIDDISH*!)

RELATE CAREFULLY *ANALYZE* EVERY REFERENCE FOR COROLLARIES TO YOUR *PERSONAL* EXPERIENCE. USE THE *DEWEY DECIMAL SYSTEM*.

GUFFAW OBSERVE THE "GETTING IT" PHENOMENON AS IT SIGNALS THE *STOMACH* & *FACIAL* MUSCLES TO GO INTO SPASM. NOW YOU MAY *LAUGH* BRIEFLY.

A YUPPIE *Meditates*

CUISINART

MM..THAT'S BETTER--

I THINK I'LL GO WITH THE *6 MONTH C.D.*

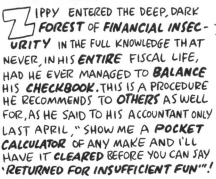

YES, WE'VE COME A LONG WAY FROM **BILL HALEY** & THE **COMETS** TO **RONALD REAGAN** & THE **MULTIPLE CLUSTER WARHEADS!**

WE'RE THE **EXPLODING INFANT** GENERATION!

NOW PAY CLOSE ATTENTION TO THESE **LIFESTYLE OPTIONS** FOR YOUR **18** TO **49** PRIME PURCHASING AGE GROUPS!!

CAN DO! I'M DEMOGRAPH-ICALLY **COR-RECTED!**

YOUR IDEAL LIFE CYCLE

JOIN THE RACE

BE A NEAT TEEN

HAVE A LITTLE FUN

ARRANGE FOR AN INEXPENSIVE FUNERAL

GO FOR THE BIG TICKET ITEMS

REPRODUCE

GET MARRIED

YIELD

CHOOSE YOUR IMAGE

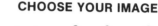

AVERAGE   NORMAL   TYPICAL

CHOOSE YOUR AUTOMOBILE

FORD   CHEVY   FORD

CHOOSE YOUR ATTACHE CASE

TOO SMALL   TOO LARGE   JUST RIGHT

STOP

FAME and FORTUNE
MAKE THE OTHER GUY WORK FOR YOU

CORROSIVE + [wine] + [bombs]

+ [bible] + [person] = [$ money bag]

LEISURE TIME
SAFE OUTLETS FOR REAL FEELINGS

FINE ORIENTAL DINING   CROSS-COUNTRY TELEVIEWING

OVERDUE BRIDGEWORK   PED X-ING

GOLF   BREAK-DANCING   TARGET PRACTICE

RANDOM ACTIVITIES 5

THE NEW PATRIOTISM

The **NEW PATRIOTISM** IS NOTHING LIKE THE **OLD PATRIOTISM**..IT'S UPSCALE, **STYLE**-CONSCIOUS AND WEARS TOPSIDERS ON THE WEEKENDS. HERE'S HOW TO BE PART OF IT.

GO LUTHERAN CONVERT IMMEDIATELY. LUTHERANS ARE **HIP**, ADVOCATE A STRONG NATIONAL DEFENSE & HAVE THE BEST **PICNICS**.

NO **RUSSIAN'S** GOING TO INVADE MY HIGH SCHOOL!

GO P.T.A. JOIN YOUR LOCAL **P.T.A.** EVEN IF YOU HAVE NO CHILDREN. MEETINGS ARE AN EXCELLENT PLACE TO **NETWORK** WITH OTHER INSULAR TYPES.

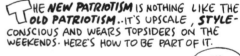

GO QUIETLY IF YOU **MUST** DISPLAY THE **FLAG**, DO IT DISCREETLY. A SMALL, 4" x 6" SIZE PLACED IN A HOLDER NEXT TO THE **VCR** WILL DO.

GOSHES! I'M **MAD**!

SOMETIME AFTER THE LAST **ATOMIC WAR** --

GOSHES! I'M THE ONLY ONE LEFT!!

UH-OH! MY **ROBOT** TOYS GOT ALL **GUCKY** FROM A NUCLEAR FIRESTORM..

WANHHHH!

RANDOM ACTIVITIES 6

THE JOYS OF PET OWNERSHIP

*T*OO MANY OTHERWISE LIKEABLE PEOPLE OWN EITHER A **CAT** OR A **DOG**. ZIPPY FEELS THAT LIFE WOULD BE MUCH IMPROVED WITH A MORE **UNUSUAL** PET AROUND THE HOUSE...

THE MOLE BRING A **MOLE** INTO YOUR HOME AND THE **FUN** BEGINS!! THEY CAN **SIT, RELAX, SLEEP & BURROW**...BITING IS NO PROBLEM.

MY MOLE IS WOUNDED.. WILL YOU HELP?

THE WOLVERINE THESE AMBI-TIOUS CREATURES MAKE WONDERFUL DOOR-TO-DOOR **SALES REPS**. WIN A **BIKE, DOLL** OR FULL YEAR'S SUPPLY!

THE KNEADED ERASER THE **ULTIMATE** PET..WILL BEG, FETCH, ROLL OVER AND REMOVE UNSIGHTLY STAINS FROM **BRISTOL BOARD**.

Dr. Marvin LIPSCHITZ "HE CARES"

IT'S A LIVING.

SEND IN THE NEXT **WIMP**, NURSE.

YES, DR.

DOC, I'M IN **LOVE** WITH A CARTOON CHARACTER!

YEH? WHICH ONE?

IT'S THAT BABY- "MARVIN.." WHAT SHOULD I DO?

CHANGE YOUR DIAPERS.

CHANGE MY DIAPERS? IS THAT **ALL**?

NO.. **DO** SOMETHING ABOUT THAT **HAIR**!!

NEW YORK — AFGHAN-ISTAN
BOMB — THE KOREAN WAR

IT SHOWS UP FOR SOME IN THEIR **MID-THIRTIES**.. FOR OTHERS, AROUND **FORTY-TWO**... FOR **OTTO GEVERTZ**, IT COMES EVERY **WEDNESDAY** AT THREE FIFTEEN ---

IDENTITY CHAMBER 707

IDENTITY CHAMBER 705

IDENTITY CHAMBER 703

PLACE ILLUSIONS HERE

I..I.. JUST WANNA BE ME!

SURE, SURE, OTTO...WE "**DIG**" YOU..

DR. **MARVIN LIPSCHITZ** — CRISIS THERAPIST AND **STYROFOAM** PRODUCTS DEALER: HIS CLIENTS INCLUDE A VERITABLE **WHO'S WHO** OF **BEATNIK** POETRY..THEY **ALL** COME TO THE "TOO MUCH TO THINK TANK & RECOVERY UNIT, INC." **EVENTUALLY**...

LISTEN, OTTO --- WHILE YOU'RE HERE YOU NEED ANY **STYRO-FOAM PACKAGING**?! REPRESENT A QUALITY LINE...

NO THANKS DOC..I JUST NEED TO KNOW **WHO** I AM, **WHY** I'M HERE &, LIKE, **WHERE** I CAN COP AN ATTITUDE--

OKAY, BABE.. SIT HERE.. & MAKE YOUR MIND A **COMPLETE** BLANK..

DOC, YOU'RE A BEAUTIFUL **DUDE**..

OUTSIDE--

BELA LUGOSI IS MY CO-PILOT..

YES? **WHO** ARE **YOU**?

I'M NOT **SURE**.. LAST WEEK, I THOUGHT I WAS **JUDY GARLAND**!!

E'VE HAD THE *JIMI HENDRIX EXPERIENCE*..WE'VE ENDURED THE *BOY GEORGE EXPERIENCE*..ZIPPY SAYS WE ARE NOW READY FOR THE *HUGH BEAUMONT EXPERIENCE.*

1. *CONCENTRATE* ON THE FRONT PAGE OF THE NEWSPAPER (NEVER UNFOLD, NEVER OPEN).

2. *COPE* WITH THE POLITENESS OF *EDDIE HASKELL*.. (COUNT TEN & REMAIN CALM).

3. *UNDERSTAND* WHAT IT MEANS TO *"BE EXCUSED".* (ALWAYS SAY YES, DON'T ASK WHY).

A GOOD, *FICTIONAL* RELATIONSHIP IS *ONE* THING, BUT APPLYING THE LESSONS WE LEARN FROM THE *CLEAVERS* TO THE *HOME FRONT* IS QUITE ANOTHER--

ZIPPY'S OWN *NUCLEAR FAMILY* HAS BEEN SUMMONED FROM THEIR LUXURIOUSLY APPOINTED, FUR-LINED *FALLOUT SHELTER* FOR A TOUCHING REUNION--

RANDOM ACTIVITIES 7

SEEING THINGS

..I WAS A TEENAGE BEATNIK

DETOUR 8

40

THE STORY OF LIFE

FOUR BILlion years back this crazy amoeba (Sid) wiggles out of the ooze and sets up house somewhere near Newark.

Little did the nutty little microorganism realize that, like, eons later Dwight D. Eisenhower and Pat Benatar would inhabit the earth, making war, preventing inflation and looking cool for adolescent boys on a bi-coastal, postnuclear cable hookup.

But let's get back to the dinosaurs. Without these cats, there would be no Denny's—Always open, some dinners not available in your area.

King Arthur was no rectangle. The Chinese gave us spaghetti but now they want to do the Funky Chicken with your daughter. Real estate values continued to rise during the Dark Ages, slowed temporarily by famine, pestilence and plague. All of this turned out to be great material for Henny Youngman some epochs later.

And what if Abbot and Costello had done Rosemary's Baby? The sixties never would have happened. We'd still be living in Eskimo sod huts, 75 miles from Nome. If only my man Sid had known he would be responsible for Andy Rooney's adenoidal platitudes, like, he never would have subdivided.

End.

© 1986 OTTO ("Otto") GEVERTZ

OTTO'S BRILLIANT, CONCISE WORK SPAWNS COUNTLESS **IMITATIONS** AND SPIN-OFFS...THERE'S THE 2-PAGE **"CAN'T WEIGHT"** DIET, THE 2-PAGE **TELEPHONE DIRECTORY** & EVEN THE 2 MINUTE **RELATIONSHIP**...

HI THERE, BIG BOY... I ENJOYED MYSELF. GET THE KIDS READY FOR SCHOOL, WILL YOU?

IT'S YOUR TURN TO TAKE OUT THE GARBAGE!

OK, BUT I GET THE HONDA & THE PASTA MAKER.

WE'VE GOTTA DO THIS AGAIN REAL SOON...

'BYE HARRY.

IT'S LARRY.

WHATEVER.

Have You HEARD

by LIZ HUDNUT

A GOOD BEAT If it's like, a "happening scene" or strictly "from Nowheresville", two page beatnik novelist Otto Gevertz is sure to know. No one who's anyone will do a thing this week without consulting Otto's "In and Out" list.

Well, busy Lizzie obtained a copy while going through the trash outside the lush, private offices of Michael Jackson's secretive younger brother, Sleazelle. I know this means no more invites to the "Pirates of the Caribbean" from Michael, but here it is. Read it and leap.

HUNGARIANS: Take time to taste the goulash. There are parts of Budapest as yet unexplored by modern man.

ED NORTON'S HAT: Don't sit on it, he just had it *blocked*. Notice the brim as it seems to *follow* you around the room.

SCHLIBBITZ: This is a board game that will soon be in short supply. If you haven't seen *every* episode of "Quincy", you can't play.

Nowhere

LAYERED SLEEVES: If we were meant to wear these things the Big Daddy would have given us segmented shoulders.

INDOOR PLANTS: They drip and make you feel guilty when they die. You wouldn't put your barcalounger on the *lawn*, would you?

SCULPTURED SLIPPERS: Did you know people wore funny slippers in 55 A.D., just before the decline of the Roman Empire?

HEAT-SEEKING MISSILES: Better we should spend sixty billion dollars a year on heat-seeking *woodchucks* and *squirrels*.

Happening

INDIVIDUALLY WRAPPED CHEESE SLICES: Keep a few in your wallet for easy access. Like, take me to your *liederkranz!*

SMURFS: These groovy little blue critters teach Johnny and Janey about total concept marketing and copyright law.

LOWER LIP FOLIAGE: With this face fur, you can convince *anyone* you're a jazz buff. Talk Diz, Satch in utter confidence.

'59 CHEVY TAIL LIGHTS: Drive down the canyons of your mind and park in the driveway of your nasal passages.

BIG BUCKLES: Just remember this timely maxim: the *smaller* the higher brain functions, the *bigger* the belt buckle.

HIDDEN PSYCHIC POTENTIAL: Keep it hidden. Nobody really wants to know you left your body and visited Buffalo.

JUST THEN, SOMEWHERE NEAR **SOUTHHAMPTON**, LONG ISLAND--

ACTUALLY, I KIND OF LIKE SCULPTURED SLIPPERS-- ED

ME, TOO!

..BUT I WOULDN'T WANT TO CONTRIBUTE TO THE DECLINE OF CIVILIZATION!

YOU'VE GOT A POINT--

RANDOM ACTIVITIES 8

PLACES NOT TO GO IN NEW HAVEN

WHEN NEXT TRAVELING TO EXCITING **NEW HAVEN,** CONNECTICUT, ZIPPY RECOMMENDS GETTING WITHIN ABOUT **2** BLOCKS OF THESE LOCALES BUT NOT ACTUALLY VISITING THEM.

BLIMPIE BASE 21 THIS WAS THE 21ST OF SEVERAL HUNDRED "SUBMARINE SANDWICH" EATERIES SPREAD THROUGHOUT THE NORTHEAST. **BLIMPIE** WAS FIRST TO OFFER UNLIMITED **LETTUCE.**

BOB'S BULKY BURGER BOB BILLED HIS ½ POUNDER AS "THE HAMBURGER WITH A **COLLEGE DEGREE**".. JUST BEFORE THE DOORS CLOSED PERMANENTLY, BOB WAS DEMANDING THAT ALL CUSTOMERS REGISTER WITH THE **C.I.A.**

ALL-NITE WASH·O·ETTE ZIPPY OFTEN FREQUENTED THE WASH-O-ETTE UNTIL THEY INSTITUTED A "YOU MUST HAVE **LAUNDRY** TO WASH" POLICY AT ALL TIMES.

 ARE YOUR SOCKS KLEAN? WITH AUNT RUTH

 DO THEY NEED MENDING?

 DO THEY **REALLY** MATCH?

OR ARE YOU JUST **KIDDING** YOURSELF?

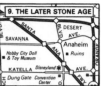

9. THE LATER STONE AGE

47

48

49

RANDOM ACTIVITIES 9

WORSHIP
TUXEDO SAM

"HE WANTS TO HELP BUT IS NOT NEEDED"

THINK ABOUT IT.

TUXEDO SAM, ZIPPY TELLS US, IS A MINOR DEITY IN THE JAPANESE "HELLO KITTY" PANTHEON.. ACCEPT THESE MAXIMS INTO YOUR HEART. WITHOUT A MOTTO* YOU'RE NOTHING!

ETERNALLY COOL THINK ABOUT IT.. THE PURITY OF AN ARCTIC EXPANSE... NO FEAR ..NO WORRY.. NO GAS OR ELECTRICITY..

TRADITIONALLY COOL "NEW-NESS" IS A THING OF THE PAST!! TUXEDO SAM MAY NOT HAVE AL-WAYS BEEN WITH US.. BUT THE IDEA OF TUXEDO SAM.. THE IDEA..

SPIFFY'S THE COOLEST THIS DICTUM IS CONFUSING UNTIL YOU REALIZE IT IS THE CONDI-TION OF SPIFFINESS THAT IS COOL. /
*ALL MOTTOS VERBATIM © SANRIO, LTD.

NANTSY, DO YOU EVER THINK ABOUT SALVA-DOR DALI?

ALL THE TIME--

DETOUR 10

IT'S BUSHMILLER TIME

YOW.!! IT'S TH' LAND THAT "DEPUTY DAWG" FORGOT.!!

Zippy subconsciously saunters into the elegant essence of Cartoon Reality.

I WONDER WHAT **ERNIE BUSHMILLER** IS UP TO TODAY

COMICS THEORY

HELLO, ERNIE --

HELLO, ZIPPY

He becomes temporarily shorter in the presence of the Great Man.

THREE ROCKS

WHAT IS **FUN**, ERNIE ?

SEARS ROEBUCK

RANDOM ACTIVITIES 10

MENTAL WORK-OUT

BURNING UNWANTED **FAT** FROM ONE'S PUCKERY **THIGHS** IS ALL WELL & GOOD BUT ZIPPY REMINDS US NOT TO FORGET THE EXCESS POUNDAGE BEHIND THOSE BABY BLUES !!

CLOWN PAINTINGS THINK ABOUT AN **ENDLESS** SIDEWALK EXHIBIT OF **CRYING CLOWN** PAINTINGS. MENTAL WT. LOSS: **7** OZ.

TH' **MIND** IS TH' PIZZA PALACE OF TH' **SOUL**

MOTEL BATHROOMS CONCENTRATE ON THE **PERSONAL BATH MAT** SUPPLIED TO EACH GUEST OF THE "MIRACLE MANOR". MENTAL WT. LOSS: **8** OZ.

HEAVY METAL HAIRCUTS THE **QUICKEST** WAY TO LOSE UNWANTED CRANIAL MATTER IS TO HAVE YOUR BARBER MAKE YOU LOOK JUST LIKE A MEMBER OF "**REO SPEEDWAGON**".. WT. LOSS: TOTAL

COMFY BOOTH

ACOUSTIC CEILING

NICE AMBULANCE

56

INTERNATIONAL HOUSE OF TOAST ••••••••••••

This fine chain of gourmet eateries features thick slices of white, wheat or rye, toasted to your order and slathered with a wide variety of coverings. The seating is plush vinyl, waitresses are outfitted in tasteful, platinum wigs. Highest starch rating. Free parking. Closed on "Toastless Tuesdays" in March.

NOSH 'N' WASH ••••••••••••••••••••

THe beDspread waS delicious And I Liked +He A-1 SauCE On iT. You put YouR SoCkS iN The hole On toP Then thinGS TO EAt come out of THe MiCrowave. SometiMES your SockS COME out of tHe MiCrowAve too BuT tHe A-1 Sauce iS also Good wiTH TiDe. PLuS you Can MEET pEoPLe & GeT MarrieD.

SENIOR SOFTEE CENTERS, U.S.A. •••••••••••••

Harsh lighting greets the over-65 crowd at the Senior Softee restaurants coast to coast. This theme is continued with the stainless steel vats of liquified rice, potatoes, macaroni and tapioca. Booths are a bit scratchy and the waitresses are all named "Nurleen". But, for the money, you seniors won't find better filler-uppers.

GENERO BURGER

BOOTHS   UNIFORMS   STARCH

Every burger you get at Genero-Burger is of a uniform size and color. Same goes for the 4 inch by ⅜ inch by ½ inch fries. They've got a branch in West Berlin but there it's all metric and darn confusing. The decor is basic black and white. Dependable, standardized beverages.

© SIOUX CITY SWINGER, INC.

GO TO **GENERO-BURGER** WHENEVER I'VE HAD A SCUFFLE WITH THE SPOUSE. IT'LL **NEVER** LET YOU DOWN..

DON'T ASK

TOPPINGS

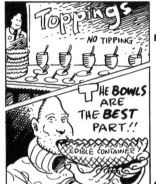

Toppings — NO TIPPING

THE BOWLS ARE THE **BEST** PART!!

EDIBLE CONTAINER

BOOTHS   UNIFORMS   STARCH

THE tHICKENERS were rich ANd StuRdY. I recommend THE FD&C ReD dYE #32 WITH SOME UNPrePaRed MUSTaRd SAUCE & NO ONE PUTS ON A beTTer PreservaTivE BUffet. MOST tOPPINGS aRe AdmINIStered orALLY but YOU do HavE a choice. effects AReN't visible foR 9 to 10 DAYs.

FIBRE-ON-A-STIK

BOOTHS   UNIFORMS   STARCH

The appeal of this place eludes me. I couldn't find no meat, no sauces, no side dishes and no flavor pouches anywhere on the limited menu. All they got is fibre and tidy washrooms. In a place like this, it's *important* to have tidy washrooms. I did a *lot* of washin' after my meal of bran cakes and dried gluten loaf.

© SIOUX CITY SWINGER, INC.

THIS IS ONE OF THEM **ORGANIC** STYLE OUTLETS WHERE EVERYTHING'S DONE BY **VOLUNTEERS**.. YOU GOTTA BRING YOUR OWN **STICKS**..!

THE ROAD TOAD

ROAD TOAD

DON'T KNOW EXACTLY **WHAT** I WAS SERVED AT TH' **ROAD TOAD** BUT I **DO** KNOW IT HAD 4 SMALL LEGS!!

BOOTHS   UNIFORMS   STARCH

You KNOW wHEN YOU're DrivING aLONG THE fREEWAY ANd YOU SEE STUff wiTH FuR THAT's DEAd? WELL, if iT'S waRM, THEY BriNG It HErE ANd PUT iT IN A CASSEROLE. WouLD YOU EAT iT? THIS IS HOW +HE WAITERS LooK

RANDOM ACTIVITIES II

SOLVE THESE
MURDERS

A LITTLE KNOWN SERIES OF UNSOLVED **MURDERS** HAS PLAGUED A BIG CITY POLICE DEPARTMENT FOR YEARS.. THE SENSELESSNESS OF THE CRIMES IS MATCHED ONLY BY ZIPPY'S INVOLVEMENT IN THE CASE.

THE PUZZLE? FOUR ELDERLY BACHELORS-ALL FOUND DEAD IN THEIR BEDROOMS... NEXT TO EACH GEEZER, A PILE OF FRESHLY WASHED **BATH TOWELS**--

DUM-DA-DUM-DUM.

THE CONNECTION? A SHAPELY WAITRESS AT THE "SENIOR SOFTEE CENTER" DATED EACH VICTIM ONCE AND GOT THEM TO SIGN UP FOR EXPENSIVE ATTIC INSULATION THRU A FRIEND'S BUSINESS..

THE SOLUTION? ZIPPY IS POSITIVE THE OLD GENTS WERE **KGB** AGENTS WHO COMMITTED SUICIDE BY BURYING THEIR NOSES IN FRESHLY WASHED BATH TOWELS TO EMBARASS THE POLICE. HE'S **WRONG** BUT STILL COLLECTED A LARGE CONSULTING FEE.

DETOUR 12 — ATTENTION SPAN

RANDOM ACTIVITIES 12

ASK ZIPPY

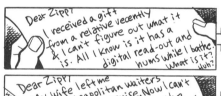

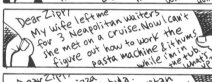

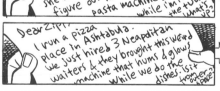

DETOUR 13

THE ANATOMY OF CUTENESS

BEFORE WE TACKLE ZIPPY'S **QUEST** FOR **CUTENESS**, LET'S EXAMINE THE WHOLE CUTENESS PROCESS--

O.K.!

LET'S LOOK AT THE 3 **PROTOTYPES**...

MAN **WOMAN** **FROG**

CUTIFICATION IS THE FINAL STAGE IN THE TRANSFORMATION FROM **INDIVIDUAL CHARACTER** TO **UNIVERSAL BULB-HEAD**...

GRIM REALITY   **SEMI-CUTE**   **CUTE**   **TERMINALLY CUTE**

CUTENESS INVOLVES **OVER-SIMPLIFICATION** OF THE FEATURES, A RELIANCE ON **CIRCLES** & **"BEAN"** SHAPES & AN OVER-ALL **"WALL-EYED"** LOOK.

GRIM REALITY   **SEMI-CUTE**   **CUTE**   **TERMINALLY CUTE**

BASIC TO THE ENTIRE PROCEDURE IS THE **REGRESSION** TO A BLAND INFANTILISM WHICH CAN BE CHEAPLY DESIGNED & **MASS-PRODUCED**..

GRIM REALITY   **SEMI-CUTE**   **CUTE**   **TERMINALLY CUTE**

66

NOW, YOU MAY SAY, "**'TWAS EVER THUS**" OR "**SUCH IS THE WAY OF CUTENESS**" — BUT YOU'RE MISTAKEN.. CUTENESS, LIKE THE TADPOLE, **EVOLVES** EVER ONWARD. AS EACH **DECADE** SLIPS BY, CUTENESS GETS **CUTER**.. SOMETIME IN **1997**, WE MAY **ALL** BE SQUEEZABLY SOFT—

I'M GETTING PUFFY!

The **THIRTIES** CUTENESS AS WE KNOW IT WAS JUST GETTING ITS START IN THE **1930s**..TURN O' THE CENTURY GRAPHIC STYLES STILL PREDOMINATED—

The **FORTIES** THE TENSIONS OF **WORLD WAR II** WERE ASSUAGED WITH A COMFORTING, VAGUELY **SEXUAL** KIND OF COY CUTENESS—

"RONI MAC" © AMERICAN BEAUTY MACARONI CO.

"JOHNNY" © PHILIP MORRIS, INC.

The **FIFTIES** THE FEISTY 'FIFTIES GAVE US **COCKY CUTENESS** AND MARK THE CULMINATION OF THE **CARICATURE** FORM.. A CUTENESS WATERSHED..

The **SIXTIES** THE **DECADENT PERIOD** BEGINS WITH THE POST-NUCLEAR, "**TWIST-O-RAMA**" STYLE SO POPULAR WITH LARGE CORPORATIONS..

"BLATZ MAN" © BLATZ BEER OF MILWAUKEE

"SONY BOY" © SONY CORPORATION

The **SEVENTIES** "**PSYCHO-CUTENESS**" MADE ITS DEBUT IN THE 'SEVENTIES, PERHAPS AS A DELAYED RESPONSE TO THE MANSON SLAYINGS—

The **EIGHTIES** ALL **STYLE** WITHOUT SUBSTANCE, THE 'EIGHTIES AT LAST GAVE CUTENESS **RESPECTABILITY**..THIS **PIG** WILL SOON RULE OUR COUNTRY!!

"LI'L SOFTEE" © ZEE TOILET TISSUE

"ZASHIKIBUTA" © SANRIO LTD.

YOU'RE NEXT!!

YES, AS HACKNEYED, REPUGNANT AND CLOYING AS IT MIGHT BE, CUTENESS **IS** A HALLOWED **CULTURAL TRADITION**.. THOSE RENAISSANCE BOYS MAY HAVE HAD THEIR SISTINE CHAPEL, ZIPPY, BUT **WE'VE** GOT "L'IL MISS SOFTEE," "CAP'N CRUNCH" & THE "KEEBLER ELF"!!

HOW'S THIS?

YOU'RE ON YOUR **WAY**, ZIP!! NOW LET'S MAKE THE TRANSFORMATION **TOTAL**!! AND DON'T FORGET: SOME ARE **BORN** TO CUTENESS, SOME **ACHIEVE** CUTENESS & OTHERS HAVE CUTENESS **THRUST UPON THEM**!!

HELLO. MY NAME IS "ZEE-PEE"!!

"ZEE-PEE" © GRIFFCO INT'L. LTD.

RANDOM ACTIVITIES 13

UNDERSTANDING PEDS

"**P**EDS" OR **PICTOGRAMS**, AS THEY ARE OFFICIALLY CALLED, INCREASINGLY POPULATE THE PUBLIC LANDSCAPE..WHAT DO THEY WANT?

DEAR, WHAT WAS THAT SIGN TRYING TO TELL US?

NO TWISTING THIS SIGN INDICATES THAT DOING THE "TWIST" BY THE ROADSIDE IS **FORBIDDEN**.

DON'T CROSS ME!

REST STOP AHEAD?

YANKEE GO HOME?

STOP: STEVE MARTIN FILM

THIS SIGN WARNS OF YET ANOTHER EFFORT BY THE FORMER DISNEYLAND EMPLOYEE.

WATCH OUT FOR SMALL GIRLS ENTERING SAUNAS WITH BAGGAGE HANDLERS

YOU SEE THESE **ALL** OVER MINNESOTA..

STORMY Romance

I MUST HAVE HIM!!

GOLLY!

HIS **HOT**, INSISTENT LIPS PRESSED ON MINE--

DARLING-- IS THAT YOU?

MY LOVE!

OH, **HENRY!**

SIGH..

68

SOCIO-POLITICAL TURMOIL

ZIPPY AWOKE THE NEXT MORNING, (HE SPENT THE NIGHT IN A "FLUFF-AIRE" DRYER) RESTORED TO HIS ORIGINAL CONDITION..

I GUESS IT WAS ALL A **DREAM** --OR AN EPISODE OF **HAWAII FIVE-O**...

"I THOUGHT I'D GRAB A DEVIL DOG & CALL A FEW DOZEN **TOLL FREE** NUMBERS -"

BUT THEN **THEY** WALKED INTO HIS LIFE.. & IT WOULD **NEVER** BE THE SAME AGAIN --

WELL, AT LEAST NOT UNTIL NEXT **FLAG DAY**..

OF COURSE I'm **PRO-FAMILY**, PAM.. AND I ALSO FAVOR ABAN-DONING **DETENTE!**

OH **PAM**, I KNOW YOU'RE **BORN AGAIN** AND SUPPORT TACTICAL **NUCLEAR WEAPONS** DEPLOYMENT FOR WESTERN EUROPE, BUT **WHAT'S** YOUR POSITION ON **PARAMILTARY SURVIVALISM??**

TERI IS SO **NAIVE**... WHY CAN'T SHE UNDERSTAND THAT PEOPLE LIKE **JERRY FALWELL** & **JESSE HELMS** JUST DON'T GO **FAR ENOUGH??**

ERI LAUNCHED AN EMOTIONAL **ARSENAL** OF SUCH MEGATONNAGE THAT PAM'S SECRET **LIBERAL LEANINGS** WERE LAID BARE!!

YOU WERE JUST **FAKING** ULTRA-CONSERVATISM!!

I'M NOT OLD ENOUGH TO HEAR THIS--

SOB!! I THOUGHT I'D MEET CUTE, REPRESSED, **UPWARDLY MOBILE BOYS** IF I HUNG OUT WITH YOU! I'M SO ASHAMED! I HOPE THE **SANDINISTAS** WILL TAKE ME BACK AGAIN!

ZIPPY, DID ANYONE EVER TELL YOU YOU RESEMBLE ►EDWIN MEESE?

IS THIS GOING TO INVOLVE **RAW** HUMAN ECSTASY?

HERE'S MY **PHONE** NUMBER-- WHEN YOU'RE READY FOR **MARRIAGE**, GIVE ME A CALL--

MY BOUDOIR IS **LEAD-LINED!!**

SIGH-- JUST LIKE **PHYLISS SCHLAFLY'S!!**

BYE BYE..

RANDOM ACTIVITIES 14

ARE YOU STILL AN ALCOHOLIC?

...THANKS..I FEEL BETTER JUST KNOWING IT'S **THERE**..

ZIPPY NEVER ACTUALLY **TRIED** ANY OF THESE **HANGOVER CURES** BUT HE SAYS "YOU DON'T HAVE TO BE A KOREAN BELL-HOP TO SELECT A FRUITY RIESLING..."

TOOTH OF THE NEWT BLEND 3 OZ.

PISTACHIO LIQUER WITH 2 TSP. **CORNSTARCH**. ADD A JIGGER OF **CHUTNEY**, SHAKE & SERVE.

I'M NOT EVEN A LICENSED PHYSICIAN!

MILLMAN'S REVENGE TO A CAN OF UNCOOKED **CREAM** OF **MUSHROOM SOUP**, STIR IN ONE PART **D-ZERTA** BUTTERSCOTCH MIX AND TWO PARTS **OUZO**. GARNISH W/ BRAN BUDS.

VELVET HACKSAW INTO A CUP OF BOILING WISHBONE **FRENCH DRESSING**, POUR 2 OZ. **DRAMBUIE**, A DOLLOP **COTTAGE CHEESE**, 2 CLOVES, A WING & 3 **PRAYERS**...

COAST TO COAST KIX

HOW'S **BUSINESS**?

FUN 3¢

AT **THIS** LOCATION? NOT SO GOOD..

HUH?

BUT WITH **612** BRANCHES NATIONALLY I GROSS A CLEAN **QUARTER MILL** A WEEK AFTER TAXES!!

FUN 3¢

I'M ALSO CAROL **CHANNING!**

DETOUR 15 — ZIPPY'S FAMOUS FUN CHAIN

FUN: DOES IT COME FROM CANADA? CAN IT BE FREEZE-DRIED? THE SCIENTIFICALLY ACCURATE CHART BELOW WAS PREPARED BY ZIPPY & A GROUP OF RECOGNIZED EXPERTS CHOSEN FROM A RANDOM SAMPLING OF JEHOVAH'S WITNESSES LIVING IN DAYTON, OHIO.

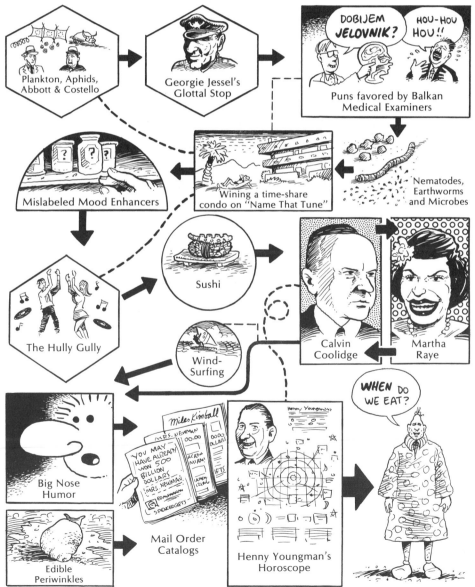

73

ENDANGERED FUN: SINCE FUN COMES TO US THROUGH A COMPLEX WEB OF INTER-DEPENDENT ELEMENTS, TAMPERING WITH **ONE** OF THOSE ELEMENTS CAN AFFECT THE **ENTIRE** CHAIN. WHAT WOULD HAVE HAPPENED IF **HENNY YOUNGMAN** NEVER EXISTED?

WITHOUT HENNY YOUNG-MAN, **MANY** CULTURAL ARTIFACTS WOULD **NOT** BE WITH US TODAY--

TORN T-SHIRTS $49.95

NEW JERSEY MALLS

ALUMINUM UNDERWEAR

HENNY

L. RON HUBBARD

WHO'S CAROL **CHANNING?**

MARRIAGE OF TINY TIM AND MISS VICKIE

MINIATURE GOLF

PANTY RAIDS

"HOW TO STUFF A WILD BIKINI"

RANDOM ACTIVITIES 15

DISPOSABLE INCOME

YOUR WALLET → K-MART

YOUR BANK → THEIR BANK

ARAB OIL PROFITS → YOUR WALLET

ZIPPY HAS A THEORY: **MONEY** IS LIKE CHICKEN **SALAD**·· IT SHOULD BE SPREAD LIBERALLY ON EVERYTHING IT COMES NEAR—

HARD-EARNED CASH AS YOUR **EARNINGS** INCREASE SO MUST YOUR **SPEND-ING.** NEVER KEEP CASH AROUND THE HOUSE. IT'S SAFER IN THE TILL OF ANY K-MART OR J.C. PENNEY'S..

MY SOCKS ARE FEDERALLY INSURED !!

LIFE SAVINGS THE ONLY OFFIC-IALLY RECOGNIZED PURPOSE OF **SAVING** IS **SPENDING**·· IF YOU DON'T HAVE ANY LIFE SAVINGS OF YOUR **OWN**, BORROW SOMEONE ELSE'S & DISPOSE OF IT INSTANTLY.

ALL THE MONEY IN SWISS BANK ACCOUNTS PRESS YOUR CONGRESSMAN TO PASS LEGISLA-TION REQUIRING ALL THIS CASH BE SPENT BY **YOU** DURING ONE WILD WEEKEND IN ATLANTIC CITY.

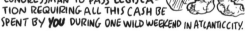

STREAM OF **CONSCIOUSNESS**

JUMP!

WATER IS WET!

AIR IS DRY!

I NOTICE THESE THINGS !!

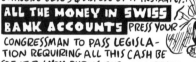

BACK TO BASICS

DROP A **BRICK**, IT FALLS TO THE GROUND.. PUT YOUR **FOOT** IN A **PUDDLE**, IT COMES OUT DRIPPING.. A FIRE WILL BE **HOT**.. ICE WILL BE **COLD** AND THE **BEDROOM** WILL ALWAYS NEED **VACUUMING**. THESE **PHENOMENA** WE ALL TAKE FOR GRANTED--

I DON'T KNOW **WHAT** IT IS, BUT IT'S **MINE!!**

SHADOW

FOR **ZIPPY**, THEY ARE A SERIES OF **STARTLING REVELATIONS**---

SIR?.. SIR? ARE YOU **ALL RIGHT?**

XMAS CLUB

ASK ABOUT OUR I.R.A.S

IT'S O.K.--

I JUST REALIZED I WAS **BREATHING**..

..BUBBLES.. ALL OF A SUDDEN-- ..**BUBBLES!!**

PARDON ME, AM I SPEAKING **ENGLISH?**

NO, **SWAHILI**.. HEY, GO BOTHER SOMEONE **ELSE**, HUH, PAL?

AVOCADO 49¢ ea.

TOMATO 99¢

OH MY **GOD**--THE **SUN** JUST FELL INTO **YANKEE STADIUM!!**

YANKEE STADIUM

75

CONCEPTS AROUND WHICH ALL HUMAN BEHAVIOR REVOLVE DO NOT EXIST IN THE NORMAL SENSE FOR ZIPPY... HE PROCESSES **EXPERIENCE** AND **SENSATION** STRICTLY IN TERMS OF ARTIFICIALLY FLAVORED **JELLY DONUTS**..

WHO BUYS LASER ART?

*See pg. 125

MONDO-REVERSO

EYEWEAR: THE LAST FRONTIER

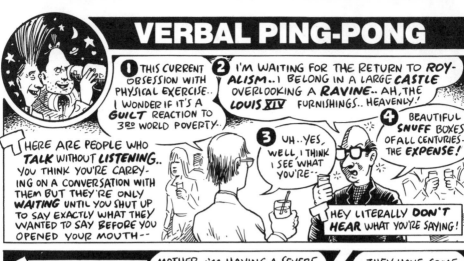

VERBAL PING-PONG

❶ THIS CURRENT OBSESSION WITH PHYSICAL EXERCISE.. I WONDER IF IT'S A *GUILT* REACTION TO 3RD WORLD POVERTY..

❷ I'M WAITING FOR THE RETURN TO *ROYALISM*..I BELONG IN A LARGE *CASTLE* OVERLOOKING A *RAVINE*.. AH, THE *LOUIS XIV* FURNISHINGS.. HEAVENLY!

❸ UH..YES, WELL, I THINK I SEE WHAT YOU'RE—

❹ BEAUTIFUL *SNUFF* BOXES OF ALL CENTURIES.. THE *EXPENSE!*

HERE ARE PEOPLE WHO *TALK* WITHOUT *LISTENING*.. YOU THINK YOU'RE CARRYING ON A CONVERSATION WITH THEM BUT THEY'RE ONLY *WAITING* UNTIL YOU SHUT UP TO SAY EXACTLY WHAT THEY WANTED TO SAY BEFORE YOU OPENED YOUR MOUTH—

HEY LITERALLY *DON'T HEAR* WHAT YOU'RE SAYING!

THE SAME PHENOMENON OCCURS WHEN DISCUSSING MATTERS OF A *PAINFUL, PERSONAL* NATURE WITH ONE'S PROGENITORS—

MOTHER, I'M HAVING A SEVERE *IDENTITY CRISIS*..I WITHDREW MY *I.R.A.* ACCOUNT & SPENT IT ALL ON *ITALIAN SHOES*—

THEY HAVE SOME *VERY GORGEOUS* STYLES ON SALE AT KINNEY'S HERE IN TAMPA..

SPOTTING ALIEN BEINGS

I'M *SORRY,* I CAN'T REVEAL MY FINANCIAL HOLDINGS TO A *CREATURE* FROM *OUTSIDE* MY OWN SOLAR SYSTEM—

HOW DID YOU GUESS?

THE *WIDE LAPELS*—THEY'RE A DEAD GIVE-AWAY!!

ALIEN BEINGS HAVE MOVED AMONG US SINCE JUNE 24, 1947. HERE ARE A FEW HANDY HINTS ON HOW TO *FIND* THEM, *TAG* THEM AND *SELL* THEM USED CARPETS..

I.R.S. TAX AUDITOR

YOU CAN ASSUME MOST *STEREO SALESMEN* ARE "NOT OF THIS WORLD"..

CHEAP DYNEL TOPPER COVERING TELL-TALE ALIEN DOME—

TYPICAL VENUTIAN

OF COURSE, THERE'S ALWAYS THE OLD "*EAR* PROTRUDING FROM THE *HAIR*" CHARACTERISTIC..

I CAN CONTROL ALL MODEM OPERATIONS USING ONLY A MONOLITHIC DIGITAL LOOP INTERFACE!!

AND, INEVITABLY *ANY ONE* WHO KNOWS ANYTHING ABOUT COMPUTERS IS FROM *PLUTO*..

IF ALL ELSE FAILS, SIMPLY CHECK THE *LABEL* INSIDE THEIR COLLAR—

ULP.

ALL ALIEN GARMENTS ARE "MADE IN KOREA"..

MADE KOREA

SPEAKING OF **ALIEN BEINGS**, THERE ARE **3** COMING UP AFTER YOU, RIGHT **NOW**, ZIPPY!!

Yow!

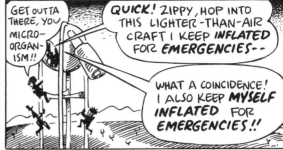

GET OUTTA THERE, YOU MICRO-ORGAN-ISM!!

QUICK! ZIPPY, HOP INTO THIS LIGHTER-THAN-AIR CRAFT I KEEP **INFLATED** FOR **EMERGENCIES**--

WHAT A COINCIDENCE! I ALSO KEEP **MYSELF INFLATED** FOR **EMERGENCIES!!**

UP, UP AND **AWAY**, TAPERED ONE!!

LAUNDRY IS THE **FIFTH DIMENSION!**

DAMN! NO RESPECT FOR CUBISM AT ALL!!

WILL THIS NEVER-ENDING SERIES OF **PLEASURABLE EVENTS** EVER CEASE?

RANDOM ACTIVITIES 17

DIALING FOR DELIRIUM

TELEVISION- ACHING ABYSS OF PASSIVITY OR KEY TO **"CHAOTIC MEDITATION"**? TEST **YOUR** RECEPTION TO THESE VIDEODDITIES!

SNOW JOKE WATCH THE **"SNOW"** ON AN OFF-THE-AIR STATION UNTIL YOU BEGIN TO SEE AND HEAR **JIMMY SWAGGART** DEBATING **LEO BUSCAGLIA'S** "BIG **HUG** THEORY"

HOW'S MY VERTICAL HOLD?

IT'S ALL IN THE KNUCKLES

SPEED VIEWING ... START BY VIEWING **5** SECONDS OF EACH AVAILABLE CHANNEL. GRADUALLY REDUCE TIME TO ½ SECOND. SOMEHOW, IT ALL BEGINS TO MAKE SENSE, SOMEHOW.

YOU PLAYED IT FOR PETUNIA..

YOU CAN PLAY IT FOR ME..

YOU'RE A PIG, BOSS.

PORKY BOGART RENT A COPY OF "CASABLANCA". NOW, USING TWO VCR'S & AN AUDIO INPUT, SUBSTITUTE **PORKY PIG'S** VOICE FOR **BOGART'S** IN ALL LOVE SCENES. IT'S KIND OF A **ZEN** THING...

Mizra-Bears

WON'T YOU SHARE IN OUR **WELT-SCHMERZ**?

GOLLY, MIZRA-BEAR WHAT'RE YOU DOING?

I'M WRITING A **SUICIDE NOTE**, CATHY...

CAN I READ IT?

WELL, IT'S MEANT TO BE READ AFTER I DIE.

THAT'S OKAY- I'LL **WAIT!!**

I got the Ding Dong
  Blues
Sadder than a dentist's
  drill
I got the Ding Dong Blues
  Had a keg of Whip 'n Chill
Look like Audrey Hepburn
  Searchin' for a diet pill

I got the Ding Dong Blues
  Dreamin' 'bout Miami Beach
I got the Ding Dong Blues
  H-bombs forty-nine cents each
Feel like Mister Rogers
  Drinkin' lots of Tab and bleach

Went to ancient Rome
Found nobody home
Cub Scouts playing Scrabble
Stole my metronome
Oh, baby, my hairstyle's obsolete
Madonna bought my building
She put my Whirlpool on the street

I got the Ding Dong Blues
    Just not having any fun
I got the Ding Dong Blues
    Headin' for oblivion
Lyin' on the sofa
    Cryin' for the Flyin' Nun

I got the Ding Dong Blues
    Head's about to bifurcate
I got the Ding Dong Blues
    Don't know what it was I ate
Could've been the sushi
    Caused me to hallucinate

One and one is four
Six and four are nine
My favorite orthodontist
Skipped to Liechtenstein
Oh, baby, I'm gloomy as Pagliacci
The only thing'll save me's
Two weeks with Liberace

I got the Ding Dong Blues
    Sufferin' from a stabbin' pain
I got the Ding Dong Blues
Guess I'm gonna go insane
Sobbin' in a phone booth
    Somewhere outside Bangor, Maine

Don't know what to do
Loquats in my shoe
Opened my fortune cookie
Said I used the wrong shampoo
Oh, baby, I'm down upon my knees
If things don't get much better
I'm gonna send out for Chinese.

RANDOM ACTIVITIES 18

BLACK HOLES

"THERE IS A *BLACK HOLE* IN EVERY ROOM IN THE ENTIRE WORLD," SAYS ZIPPY. "DON'T PUT YOUR HEAD OR LUNCH INTO ONE OF THEM IF YOU DON'T WANT TO BE VIOLENTLY SUCKED IN!"

UNDER CABINETS LOCATE THE BLACK HOLE UNDER YOUR KITCHEN CABINET. THERE IS A *CREATURE* INSIDE WHO SWALLOWS CORKS, RUBBER BANDS & DISCOUNT COUPONS

IN CLOSETS YOU WILL *NEVER*, EVER SEE YOUR JIGSAW PUZZLES OR SHELL COLLECTION AGAIN ONCE YOU PUT THEM IN THE BACK CORNER OF YOUR *HALL CLOSET*..

THE HOUSE OF REPRESENTATIVES WORST OF ALL, THERE IS A BLACK HOLE UNDER THE SPEAKER'S PODIUM IN OUR NATION'S CAPITOL WHERE ALL OF OUR HARD-EARNED *TAX* DOLLARS EVENTUALLY WIND UP.

88

RANDOM ACTIVITIES 19

HOW TO BUILD A NUCLEAR DEVICE

Did you know you can buy everything you need to build a working NUCLEAR DEVICE from a Frederick's of Hollywood catalog?

YOU'LL NEED: ONE (LARGE SIZE) "BLAZING LOVE SADDLE" WITH DUAL-ACTION, CROTCHLESS STIMULATOR RING, A HYDRO-DYNAMIC BREAST CUP & 3 JARS OF "JOY-JELL."

IT COULD SAVE YOUR MARRIAGE.

SIMPLE INSTRUCTIONS USING TWO KILOS OF ORDINARY, HIGH-GRADE PLUTONIUM & THE CONDENSER COIL FROM A TAPPAN "FROST-FREE" FREEZER, SOLDER TAB "C" TO NODULE "R-768-X".

CALL THE WHITE HOUSE ASK TO SPEAK TO A HIGH LEVEL CABINET OFFICIAL AND DEMAND AN UNCONDITIONAL END TO THE ALBANIAN GRANOLA EMBARGO.

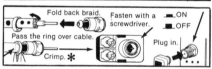
Fold back braid. Fasten with a screwdriver. Pass the ring over cable. Crimp. ON OFF Plug in.

JUST DON'T PUSH THE G-SPOT!!

90

LISTEN, CHUM.. I WANT TO **TALK** TO YOU...

IS IT ABOUT **FOOD** WITH **FUR**?

NO.. I'VE BEEN **WATCHING** YOU, BUNKY.. I SEE YOU'VE GOT QUITE A SENSE OF **HUMOR**..

YOU **KID** ME **NOT!!**

YOU KNOW WHAT THE **BASIS** OF ALL HUMOR IS, DON'T YOU, FUN-BOY??

A WIDE-EYED, INNOCENT **UNI-CORN**, POISED DELICATELY IN A **MEADOW** FILLED WITH **LILACS**, **LOLLIPOPS** & SMALL **CHILDREN** AT THE **HUSH** OF TWILIGHT??

NO, CHUM... IT'S THE **HEALTHY** NEED TO LAUGH AT THE **PAIN** & **SUFFERING** OF **JERKS** & **ASSHOLES!!**

CAPITO

TOAD TONIGHT

SAVAGE, BITING, SKEWS BI-MODALLY!!
-SIOUX CITY SWINGER

EXCUSE ME, SIR..BUT ISN'T IT **ALSO** THE RECOGNITION DEEP WITHIN OURSELVES THAT **LIFE** IS ACTUALLY..

UNICORNS **CAN** BE ANNOYING.

KEEP **OUT** OF THIS, YOU !! THIS IS A **PRI-VATE** CONVER-SATION !!

HOW'D YOU LIKE TO EXPLORE THE **HIDDEN** SHADOWS AT TH' CORE OF YOUR SOUL, PAL.. ..C'MON, YOU'RE GONNA **LOVE** THIS STUFF !!

I'M RATED **PG-34!!**

"COMEDY WITH AN EDGE"

ONE NIGHT ONLY

94

LOOK! IN HERE! MEDIA ATTENTION!!

THAT'S TH' *STAGE*, YOU BOZO! DON'T GO OUT THERE!!

CURTAIN 8 P.M.

I OUGHTA *KILL* YOU, YOU DIRTY.. YOU.. -. *HUH*?

THE *BASIS* OF ALL *HUMOR*!!

CLAP CLAP CLAP HA HA HA

HUH? ..UH.. THANK YOU.. LADIES & GERMS.. *THANK* YOU..

TELL THE ONE ABOUT THE *HIDDEN SHADOWS* AT THE CORE OF YOUR *SOUL*!!

HA HA CLAP CLAP *CLAP!*

I'M A *GENIUS!* I WANT TO DISPUTE SENTENCE STRUCTURE WITH *SUSAN SONTAG*!!

TOAD TONIGH

RANDOM ACTIVITIES 20

REFRIGERATOR MAGNETS
FOR THE '90s

THE IDEA OF GLEAMING *ACRYLIC* FOOD ATTACHED FIRMLY TO A REFRIGERATOR DOOR IS ONE THAT HAS FASCINATED HOMO SAPIENS FOR EONS. *YOU* CAN MAKE THESE IN *ANY* HI-TECH PLASTICS LAB.

-Milk
-Eggs
-Lug Nuts
-Bread

ASPARAGUS 'N BICS
THIN, TENDER TIPS ALTERNATED WITH MEDIUM POINT *BICS* WRAPPED IN A "RAW" *BACON STRIP!*

THIS ONE'S STILL *ALIVE!*

Honey-went to aerobics investing seminar

JELLO CUBES 'N WINDOW LOCKS
LIME, CHERRY & GRAPE WITH MAT FINISH ALUMINUM SECURITY DEVICES MAKE AN *URBAN* STATEMENT!

-MOVE THE BMW
-DRAIN THE Tax Shelter

LUG NUTS 'N SQUID
THE *DIETER'S* SPECIAL- REMINDS YOU TO ROTATE YOUR RADIALS EVERY TIME YOU DINE ON *CALIMARI!*

APRÈS FUN

ZIPPY, I WANT YOU TO KNOW I HAD A *WONDERFUL* TIME..

WHAT WAS IT YOU SAID *YOU* FELT LIKE?

A SET OF DECORATIVE, BAMBOO *BAR STOOLS*..

OH

Zimplicity ITSELF

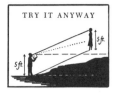
TRY IT ANYWAY

5 ft. / 5 ft.

THERE'S SOMETHING ZIPPY'S BEEN WANTING TO SAY EVER SINCE HE REALIZED HE'S AS MUCH A PART OF THE **REAL WORLD** AS **LEE IACCOCA** OR THE **SEAGRAM** BUILDING ---

I HAVE A VERY GOOD **DENTAL PLAN**.. THANK YOU.

RANDOM ACTIVITIES 21

HOW TO DRAW SHELF-LIFE

NEXT TIME YOU'RE **DOODLING** ON THE TELEPHONE SCRATCH PAD, TRY YOUR HAND AT COR- RECTLY DEPICTING MR. **SHELF-LIFE NURNEY**!!

HAIR UNIT IT WILL HELP IN DRAWING S.L.'S **COIFFURE** TO THINK OF THE END OF AN ODDLY- SHAPED **SCREWDRIVER**..

— BUY, SELL, BUY SELL, Y'KNOW WHAT I **MEAN**?

UPPER FACIAL UNIT THE **HARDWARE** THEME IS CONTINUED WITH SHELF-LIFE'S **"HATCHET-NOSE"** AND "FEARLESS FOSDICK" BONE STRUCTURE.

LIPS UNIT S.L.'S **LIPS** HAVE A "LIFE OF THEIR OWN" & PRECEDE HIM AS HE APPROACHES. THEY ARE THE ONLY **CURVILINEAR** AREAS IN HIS ENTIRE PHYSICAL MAKE- UP....

LET'S TALK BEEF

Progress of **ROCK 'n ROLL LYRICS** 1958-1986.

SPLISH, SPLASH, I WAS TAKIN' A BATH!! 1958

NEWSPAPER TAXIS APPEAR ON THE SHORE----- 1969

SPLISH, SPLASH, I WAS TAKIN' A BATH!! 1986

HEY, GOOMBA.._I'LL_ TELL YOU ABOUT _ROCK 'N ROLL_-- IT'S, YOU KNOW, YOUR BASIC _PARTY_ MUSIC.._NOVELTY_ KINDA THING.. ..JUST FOR HAVIN' A _GOOD TIME_..GET A L'IL TIPSY..

I THINK WE'RE ALONE NOW--

NO _WAY_, LOUIE..IT'S ABOUT THE _AGONY_ OF ADOLESCENCE..KIND OF A _COMFORT_ TO PRE-TEEN GIRLS WHO, LIKE, ARE MAKIN' THE MOVE FROM _GUPPIES_ TO _GONADS_..

HEY _ROCK 'N ROLL_ IS ABOUT _WARDROBE_, _HAIRSTYLE_ & _LUBRICATION_! I OUGHTA KNOW!

..BUT DO _BILLY IDOL_ & _CYNDI LAUPER_ SHARE THE _SAME LIPS?_

YOU NEVER SEE ALL _FOUR_ OF THEM TOGETHER..

I HOPE MY AUDIENCE CAN GROW WITH ME..

I'VE GOT THIS _THING_ FOR _LACE_ & _CRUCIFIXION_ ..IT'LL BE BIG FOR A WHILE, THEN I SWITCH TO _FLORAL PRINTS_ AND _ARMY BOOTS_--

IT'S LIKE A _RE-LIGIOUS THING_ BUT WITHOUT THE _GUILT_.. MASS HYSTERIA..A PLACE TO PUT ALL YOUR _HEAVIEST_ FEELINGS.. ASK YOURSELF--"SHOULD I _FEEL NICE_ OR BECOME A _REGISTERED NURSE?_"

TH' BEAT-ING OF OUR HEART IS TH' ONLY SOUND..

HEY, GOOMBA!! _"PRINCE"_ IS JUST _LIBERACE_ WITH HIS _PANTS_ DOWN.. IT'S ALL _SHOW BIZ_.. LET'S NOT GO _SOCIO-LOGICAL_, EH, PAISAN'??

IT'S _COMMER-CIALIZED_ "FOLK MUSIC"!!

A _SAFE_ WAY TO "_REBEL_"!

ARTISTIC EXPRESSION!

TH' _BEAT_ IS EVERY-THING!

PUBERTY RITES!

TH' LATEST BANDWAGON!

HEY, _GOOMBA!_

A RIP-OFF OF _BLACK_ CULTURE!

TEEN PROTEST!

HOLD IT, ROCK FANS!! IT'S TIME TO CONSULT A SPEC-IALLY PREPARED _CHART_ REJECTED BY "TIGER BEAT"!! ALSO, LET'S PAY _TRIBUTE_ TO ROD STEWART'S PHARMACIST!!

HUEY! DEWEY! LOUIE!

ZIPPY'S SPECIALLY PREPARED
MODERN MUSIC CHART

MUSICAL CATEGORY	WHAT IS THEIR MESSAGE?	WHO IS THEIR AUDIENCE?	WHAT DO THEY THINK ABOUT?	DO THEY COLLECT DISHES?	WHAT WILL THEY BE DOING IN 20 YEARS?	FASHION TIPS
POUND 'n POUT	It's all right to be a transvestite as long as you have several tatoos & drink heavily.	14-year-old boys who want to start World War Three because their parents are never home.	Ways to torture insects, getting electrocuted & how great the 70s were.	Yes.	20 years.	Everything you need is hanging in your sister's closet.
PRANCE 'n POSE	Pre-marital sex is okay if it's between consenting rock stars.	Anyone with $15.50.	Those simonized twins back in the dressing room.	Yes.	Announcing the matches on "Wrestling from Atlanta".	Imagine **Audrey Hepburn** in leatherette.
TWITCH 'n TWANG	We are all robots but some robots are more musically inclined than other robots.	Elderly art students, lawyers & other unemployable types.	Reinforced concrete, big clothes, pasta salad & civil defense manuals.	No.	Running a chain of software outlets.	Think what you could do with carpet remnants.
SWEAT 'n SQUINT	Things are pretty bad but they could be worse if you lived in **Dallas.**	Mostly former White House advisers.	Driving a car bomb through the gates of **Epcot Center.**	Yes.	Commercials for fast food restaurants in **Beirut.**	You're beautiful. Don't ever change.
SLITHER 'n SLURP	It's okay to hang out in shopping malls if you go to confession next day.	100% Scandinavian.	How to get closer to **Menudo.**	No.	Representing the fine line of **Herbalife** products.	Have you really got enough boxer shorts?
SNEER 'n STARE	Life is hard & then you make videos.	Children of permissive pharmacists.	Beer.	No.	Coming out with an exercise book.	Shave an outline of **Bullwinkle Moose** on the back of your head.
SCRATCH 'n SNIFF	Act bad, dress bad, walk bad, talk bad, **be** bad & get good tax advice.	The entire **Osmond** family including the black ones.	Li'l Catholic schoolgirls who have large sticker collections.	Yes.	Guest-hosting the **Donahue** Show.	Wear as many belts & zippers as is humanly possible.

RANDOM ACTIVITIES 22

CREATING ARTISTIC HEDGES

THERE'S SOMETHING ABOUT A **HEDGE**.. IT WANTS TO BE **SHAPED..MOLDED.. TRANSFORMED**...INTO A **FAMOUS FIGURE!**

THE SEAN PENN START WITH A **STRONG** PROFILE.. **CHARLTON HESTON** WAS A POPULAR HEDGE IN THE '50S-- BUT THIS IS **NOW!!**

CLIP ART.

THE LITTLE LULU DON'T FORGET THE OLD **ROBERT FROST** LINE: "GOOD LITTLE LULU HEDGES MAKE GOOD NEIGHBORS."

THE BABY HUEY A REAL CONVERSATION STARTER, THE **HUEY HEDGE** REQUIRES CONSTANT MAINTENANCE!!

POMADE IN JAPAN

I'D LIKE SOME **HAIR TONIC** PLEASE..

THIS **ORNAMENT FELLOW** IS NOT OF **SPORTS!!**

MIGHTY **TOOL** FOR LONESOME **CAR-BOY!**

CAN I HAVE A **FORK?**

WHIR-R-R..

100

103

RANDOM ACTIVITIES 23

KITSCH & TELL

AMERICAN CULTURE IS BEING INUNDATED WITH **KITSCH** SAY SOME OBSERVERS. AMERICAN **KITSCH** IS BEING INUNDATED WITH **CULTURE** SAYS ZIPPY--HERE ARE HIS 3 **KRITERIA** FOR **KITSCH!**

DOES IT HAVE THAT WOOD GRAIN LOOK?

IF SOMETHING CAN **LOOK** LIKE SOMETHING **ELSE**, IT WILL LOOK **BETTER** THAN WHEN IT WAS JUST **ITSELF**--

WANNA SEE MY **WILMA** TATTOO?

IS IT GORGEOUS? WHAT WERE THE **PARTHENON** OR **NIAGARA FALLS** BEFORE THE GORGEOUS "**SOUND LIGHT**" SHOWS? **RUINS** AND **WATER**!!

IS THERE A ROLE IN IT FOR BETTE MIDLER? SELF-CONSCIOUS KITSCH IS **ALMOST** BETTER THAN **NO** KITSCH AT ALL..

anything → can → HAPPeN.

DETOUR 24

THE YOW OF PHYSICS

N HIS CONSTANT QUEST FOR **FUN** AND REALLY GREAT FRESH **MOZ-ZARELLA**, ZIPPY WANTS US TO REMEMBER THAT THE **UNDERLYING** UNIVERSAL TRUTHS ARE NOT ALWAYS FOUND IN AN EPISODE OF **"MIAMI VICE"** OR ON THE MENU AT **SAMBO'S**..IN FACT, THE **TRUE** MYSTERIES OF EXISTENCE ARE EITHER COMPLETELY **NON-VERBAL** OR ONLY AVAILABLE **THURSDAYS**... HERE THEY ARE, **CLEARLY ILLUSTRATED**--

The Eternal Paradox

MATTER

ANTI-MATTER

The Space-Time Continuum

Photons, Protons, Neutrinos & Quarks on Their Day Off

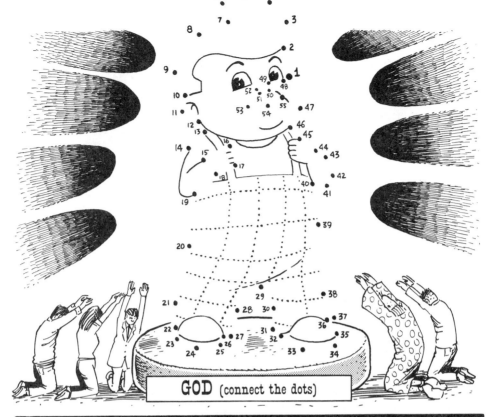

GOD (connect the dots)

RANDOM ACTIVITIES 24

THREE BIG ANSWERS

Contrary to popular belief, there **ARE PRECISE ANSWERS** to those 3 persistent questions which have puzzled humankind down through the centuries--

WHO ARE WE? We're a roving band of obscure **CLARINETISTS** who play a wedding here & a prom there and never get quite enough work to qualify for a decent pension.

Of course, I could be mistaken...

WHY ARE WE HERE? We're here to find a good quality **LINOLEUM** that matches the bathroom and will require a minimum of washing & waxing.

WHERE ARE WE GOING? We're going to an overcrowded **BEACH** on Long Island Sound where a large **WAVE** will knock us over & fill our bathing suit with gritty sand.

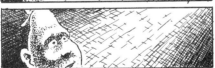

ALIENS... must register

U.S. POST OFFICE
THIS IS ALIEN REGISTRATION WEEK
GNIRP!

MUCHAS GRACIAS, SEÑOR--

WONDERFUL WORLD OF STAMPS

OH, JEEZ..

?

HEY, ED! WE GOT **ANOTHER** VARIATION ON THE ALIEN REGISTRATION GAG---

THERE'S A LOT MORE TO LIFE THAN *SUSHI* & *WIND-SURFING*!!

EMOTOSTAT-19

Far from earthly toil and strife, the creatures of *Emotostat-19* wile away their leisure *spumverds* (hours) playing *Doil-No-Web*, a game similar to our "bobbing for apples". Instead of teeth, though, the Emotostatians use (spaghetti) tongs attached to their *martobials* (foreheads) and attempt to grasp tiny pink birds squirming uncomfortably in a tureen of *staxapid* (minestrone soup). The first contestant to fall headlong into the nutrients is "sent to snuf-lib" (leaves the room). He or she is then eligible for many prizes. The *winner* is the first player who removes a bird and forces it to correctly guess the number of *xenxecks* (hairs) on a *Garmathian Skurd*. High-pitched chirping can be heard for many voitlings during an exciting game.

ROL-NAB

The inhabitants of the ice-planet *Rol-Nab* entertain themselves by tossing jars of *Vnexyl* (rubber cement) down a long tube to collide with carefully set up day-glo sponges, soaked in something like melted gorgonzola. Small boys call out scores and hose down the sponge chamber. ("Rols" grow at an alarming rate: at the end of a typical vnexyl-tossing session, several will have matured into respected sports figures, businessmen and *yazmed spinners* [AM disc jockeys].) When a score of a-5/vrR .043-7K (500) is attained, the winner goes before a panel of elders and must *ferb* (knit) orlon sweaters for each of them. Since the elders must keep their central nervous systems constantly exposed to the frigid Rol-Nabian winds, this futile exercise is the cause for much merriment.

HOSE 'EM DOWN!

HA HA!!

I WON!!

YOU DIRTY *NOGZNER*!!

FLENK!

NEW TOBLIK

To the nomadic *Turffs* of *New Toblik*, there is nothing as relaxing and enjoyable as a prolonged visit to a formica-lined rectilinear enclosure where *zunce* (single malt whiskey) is consumed during week-long *wobular* (open house) parties. Turffs of all sexes intermingle freely during these ritual gatherings, often passing out in the back seats of each other's *arsnaks* (pick-up trucks). Here the fun really goes into high gear as they race up and down the New Toblish salt flats, their small heads poking comically from the roofs of their supercharged atomic vehicles. It is said the ultimate *wobular* bash will take place when the two moons of *Krebulot* collide in 4267 A.D.

*Meathead.

CALFLORD

The inhabitants of *Calflord* are a fun-loving race of tri-peds. For the past 22 years they've been observing and imitating the people of Southern California and Florida! A typical Calflordian weekend is spent by the *slerm-nesh* (pool) reading Tab Hunter's fan mail (intercepted via laser) while debating the taco/sashimi question until somebody suggests a visit to the *Rendrick Sector* (a perfect clone of *Epcot Center* except for the yogurt pops). They talk like *Huckleberry Hound* and frolic shamelessly through fields of *rambosticia* (twist caps).

WHAT'S TH' LATEST DEVELOPMENT?

BEER IS OUT.. COOLERS ARE IN !!

REEBOKS

FEEEMB

Feeemboids spend all but one *gleeemb* (day) per *beeemb* (year) in deep anxiety and guilt. But on that day (called *Yaveeemb*) they strap powerful electro magnets to their enormous tails and romp through airport terminals attracting random metallic candy wrappers and gnawing at furniture. The tension caused by the monstrous traffic *jeeemb* (jam) on their return to the city triggers a communal release of *snazeeemb* (melted gorgonzola) which takes almost an entire beeemb to clean up, perpetuating the guilt/glut cycle.

RANDOM ACTIVITIES 25

TAILFINS ARE YOUR FRIENDS

ZIPPY BELIEVES THAT THE *TAILFINS* OF AMERICAN AUTOS OF THE LATE '50S CONTAIN *MESSAGES* SENT TO US BY THE GODS...NEXT TIME YOU PASS A '57 CHEVY, SHOW SOME RESPECT.

'59 OLDSMOBILE IF PLACED IN THE RIGHT HANDS, THE FIN ON THIS *OLDS 98* COULD BRING ABOUT BI-LATERAL NUCLEAR DISARMAMENT QUICKER THAN YOU CAN SAY "HOLIDAY SPORT SEDAN!"

PRAY TO YOUR PLYMOUTH..

'59 EDSEL ZIPPY LIKES TO SAY "IF THE *EDSEL* DID NOT EXIST, MAN WOULD HAVE TO INVENT HIM.." INSIDE EACH EDSEL TAILFIN IS A BROCHURE PREDICTING *TOFUTTI*..

'60 DODGE THIS VEHICLE WAS CLEARLY LEFT TO US FOR THE PURPOSES OF *COLONIZING* DISTANT PLANETS & CRUISING FOR *BURGERS*...

A PIN & HIS DOG

WHATEVER HAPPENED TO SPANKY McFARLAND?

HE WHOLESALED *COCA-COLA* FOR A WHILE -- HIS FIRST MARRIAGE ENDED IN DIVORCE..

ALFALFA DIED IN A QUARREL IN 1959.. *BUCKWHEAT* WAS KILLED FLYING FOOD TO BIAFRA IN '68..

TOKYO ROSE LIVES IN CHICAGO!

I HEAR SHE'S PLANNING A COMEBACK.

RANDOM ACTIVITIES 26

GUYS 'N GALLERIES

THESE RULES OF **ETIQUETTE** FOR **GALLERY OPENINGS** MAY SPARE YOU THE HARDSHIP OF FORMING AN OPINION, ONE WAY OR ANOTHER, ABOUT MODERN PAINTING OR SCULPTURE...

STUFF ON WALLS YOU CAN FIND LOTS OF THINGS TO **TALK** ABOUT AT AN OPENING..TRY **INTEREST RATES**-JUST DON'T LOOK AT THE STUFF ON THE WALLS..

I DON'T KNOW WHAT I LIKE BUT I DON'T LIKE IT.

HAVING THOUGHTS IF YOU FIND YOURSELF HAVING A **THOUGHT** ABOUT THE **ART.** REMEMBER – THE PERSON YOU'RE TALKING TO IS ALMOST **ALWAYS** THE **MOTHER** OF THE ARTIST--

BAD WHITE WINE WHEN YOUR INEVITABLE PLASTIC GLASS OF **BAD WINE** INEV-ITABLY CRACKS, IT'S TIME TO **LEAVE**...

117

  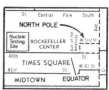

DETOUR 27 LUNCH WITH *Leona*

LISTEN, I WANT YOU TO TELL ME IF THE **SLIGHTEST THING** IS OUT OF PLACE ON THIS **TABLE**..OR ANY-WHERE **ELSE** IN THE UNIVERSE...

..THERE **WAS** ONE THING, LEONA..I GUESS I'D BETTER JUST **BLURT** IT OUT..

THIS MORNING..--THERE WAS A **MINT** ON MY **PILLOW**--

BUT THERE'S **SUPPOSED** TO BE A **MINT** ON YOUR **PILLOW**..IT'S A MARK OF TOTAL **ELEGANCE!**

OH..NOW I'M **ASHAMED.**

BUT IF YOU DON'T **LIKE** IT..THAT'S YOUR **PRIVELEGE** AS A GUEST..PARDON ME.. GET ME THE SIXTH FLOOR **MAID**..HELLO? YOU'RE **FIRED!**

SHE'S **ASS-ERTIVE**–AND SHE WAS BORN IN **FLATBUSH!**

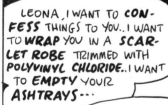

LEONA, I WANT TO **CON-FESS** THINGS TO YOU..I WANT TO **WRAP** YOU IN A **SCAR-LET ROBE** TRIMMED WITH POLYVINYL CHLORIDE..I WANT TO **EMPTY** YOUR **ASHTRAYS**...

SWEETHEART..I'VE GOT **FOURTEEN** CENTRAL AMERICANS TO DO THAT..LET ME HEAR ABOUT YOUR **COMPLAINTS**..

SHOULD I START WITH THE TIME I **SWITCHED** PERSONALITIES WITH A **BEAT-NIK** HAIR STYLIST OR MY FAILURE TO REFER FIVE **TEENAGERS** TO A GOOD **OCULIST?**

GET ME THE **EYEWEAR SHOPPE**..

--SIGH-- IT COULD HAVE BEEN SO *BEAUTIFUL*... LOVE.. COMPANION-SHIP... *ROOM SERVICE* UNTIL 1999...

I'M *DESPONDENT*... I HOPE THERE'S SOMETHING *DEEP-FRIED* UNDER THIS MINIATURE *DOMED STADIUM*---

HELLO.

WHO ARE *YOU?* AND WHY AREN'T YOU ON SALE AT *WINCHELL'S??*

DON'T YOU *RECOGNIZE* US, ZIPPY?? WE'RE YOUR *ARBITRARY DONUTS!!* YOUR QUEST IS *OVER!!*

CONGRATULATIONS! NOW SHOULD I MAKE THINLY VEILED COMMENTS ABOUT *DIGNITY*, SELF-ESTEEM AND FINDING *TRUE FUN* IN YOUR *RIGHT VENTRICLE??*

LET'S *SKIP* IT, ZIP!! JUST TAKE US WHEREVER YOUR *ANTERIOR FORNIX* LEADS YOU!!

OVER THE UNDER-TOW! *UNDER* THE OVERPASS! AROUND THE *FUTURE* AND *BEYOND REPAIR!!*

FOLLOW YOUR CARNIVAL INSTINCTS!

TOXIC SPILL

RANDOM ACTIVITIES 27

A SCARY STORY

TELL THIS *STORY* AT YOUR NEXT FAMILY REUNION, TAILGATE PARTY OR COMPANY PICNIC. IT WILL GO OVER *BIG* & MAKE YOU THE *ENVY* OF ALL, YOUNG & OLD ALIKE --

THE BEGINNING MR. *ORVILLE TWERP* OF DALLAS, TEXAS WOKE UP IN A SMALL, WHITE ROOM.. HE STARED UP AT A HARSH LIGHT & HEARD A STRANGE, OMINOUS *HUM*---

.. MY *NOSE* IS *NUMB!*

THE MIDDLE "WHAT WILL THEY *DO* WITH ME?" HE WORRIED.. "I DON'T KNOW ANYTHING ABOUT SECRET LAUNCH SITES OR THE *STAR WARS* PROGRAM.."

THE END TWO FIGURES AP-PROACHED HOLDING HORRIBLE INS-TRUMENTS OF TORTURE.. "I CONFESS! I *CONFESS!*" SCREAMED ORVILLE.. THEN A VOICE SAID "YOU MAY RINSE NOW.." & A *BIB* WAS REMOVED FROM AROUND HIS NECK....

TH' FUTURE STRETCHES BEFORE US, *ZIP*.

..I WONDER WHAT'LL HAPPEN IN TH' FIELD OF *LASER* ASSISTED MARKET ANALYSIS *50* YRS. FROM NOW..!

..I WONDER WHAT'LL HAPPEN IN A FIELD OF CHOCOLATE *BUNNIES 15* MINUTES FROM NOW..

MONO-RAIL

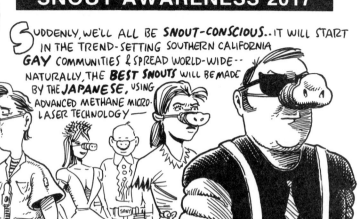

SNOUT AWARENESS 2017

OF COURSE **EVERYONE** WANTS TO KNOW WHAT WILL BE HAPPENING IN **THESE** 3 MAJOR AREAS OF SOCIAL CONCERN--

Suddenly, WE'LL ALL BE **SNOUT-CONSCIOUS**...IT WILL START IN THE TREND-SETTING SOUTHERN CALIFORNIA **GAY** COMMUNITIES & SPREAD WORLD-WIDE-- NATURALLY, THE **BEST SNOUTS** WILL BE MADE BY THE **JAPANESE**, USING ADVANCED METHANE MICRO-LASER TECHNOLOGY--

SCRIPT

SONY

POWER BATHROOMS 2039

As **VICTORIAN** ATTITUDES CONTINUE TO FALL BY THE WAYSIDE, **CORPORATE EXECUTIVES** WILL BEGIN TO TAKE IMPORTANT **MEETINGS** IN **YOUR** BATHROOM--

REMEMBER, IN 2039, **MOUSSE** & **PASTA** WILL BE AVAILABLE **ONLY** BY PRESCRIPTION !!

THIS IS **CASUAL!**

THE **DISNEY-FLEER** MERGER

IT'S A DEAL.. HAVE **MY** METHANE MICRO LASER CALL **YOUR** METHANE MICRO LASER!

SCRIPT

HOSTESS PRODUCTS 2065

& IF YOU THINK YOU'RE IN "FRESH GUYS COUNTRY" **NOW**, JUST WAIT 'TIL **2065**!!

SCRIPT

CHOSTAGES
CHOSTAGES
HIJACK-SNAX

"CHOSTAGES"
CHOCOLATE-COVERED **HOSTAGE**-SHAPED SNACK CAKES WITH **CREME SWIRL** "BLINDFOLDS"--

"SPLATZ"
THEY LOOK LIKE THEY WERE **DROPPED** FROM A GREAT HEIGHT!

Splatz

"MEDICINE BALLS"
SOFT, CHEWY AND FILLED WITH A MILD **SEDATIVE**!!

MEDICINE BALLS

Sticks 'n Scones

"STICKS 'n SCONES"
CRISPY, SOY-BASED **THROWING BISCUITS!**

MADE BY AN EXCLUSIVE METHANE MICRO-LASER PROCESS ®

DETOUR 29 — ARE WE HAVING FUN YET?

THE QUESTIONNAIRE

IS THIS A **QUIZZICAL** EXPRESSION?

Zippy's grand *tour de farce* is over but how many fun-facts-to-know-and-tell have *you* absorbed? Eyes forward? Pencils ready? Let's find out.

□FUN may be elusive and transitory but this test isn't. Choose the most appropriate response then read on to compute your FUN QUOTIENT. Hidden, yet indisputable, meaning has been attributed to your tally by Zippy and a panel of former Jehovah's Witnesses now running a "Nosh 'n Wash" on the French Riviera.

1 *You're in a vast amusement park, dressed only in a t-shirt and muk-luks. An irridescent "rubberman" offers you eternal life. Do you:*
a. Pull out a .357 Magnum and make his day.
b. Accept his offer as the music swells and a new day dawns brightly on the horizon.
c. Tell him to call your agent.
d. Suddenly wake up in Jersey City.

2 *You'd probably laugh out loud if:*
a. Someone tripped on a curb and went sprawling into a tub of marshmallow Tofutti.
b. You heard a joke with the name "Joan Rivers" in it.
c. It was revealed that Pat Sajak is not of this planet.
d. Joan Rivers tripped on a curb and went sprawling into a tub of marshmallow Tofutti.

3 *How would you rate yourself on each of the following? (E for excellent, S for satisfactory, F for so-so, U for unsatisfactory.)*
a. Knowledge of Cubism.
b. Ability to imitate Jack Palance.
c. Naugahyde perception.
d. Sex life.
e. Newspaper recycling.

4 *When a sexy friend says, "Let's go over to my accountant's and talk T-bills and tax reform all weekend!", you:*
a. Go along with the gag but bring Vaseline and Wheat Thins, just in case.
b. Call suicide prevention.
c. Say "No thanks, I'm making my bed this weekend."
d. Ponder the Smurf/Rainbow Brite controversy until you feel better about yourself.

5 *With whom do you most closely identify?*
a. Shecky Greene.
b. Marion Lorne.
c. Julio Iglesias.
d. Wilma Flintstone.
e. Your food processor.

6 *If you were stranded on a desert island for six months what would you take along? (Choose two.)*
a. A selection of nutritious Hostess products.
b. A satellite dish.
c. Edwin Meese.
d. Several Japanese shopping bags.
e. 14 acrylic refrigerator magnets.

7 *You suffer pangs of guilt and remorse when:*
a. They run out of baco-bits at the "Sizzler".
b. World War Three ravages your apartment.
c. Wayne Newton drops by unexpectedly.
d. In a fit of righteous indignation, you halt production on all teen sex comedies.

8 *For various reasons, you and Tony Randall aren't getting along. The most likely social scenario is:*
a. You send him a box of "Hello Kitty" bath accessories to patch things up.
b. You spend three weeks in Toledo, wallowing in self-pity and empty bottles of Kaopectate.
c. You dream you're in an episode of the "Odd Couple" but all you're wearing is a t-shirt and muk-luks.
d. You go for months without reading a single Beatnik poem.

I WONDER IF **ADULTHOOD** IS A REQUIRED COURSE...

9 *You witness an alien landing behind the "Wendy's" at a nearby shopping mall. You hear Steven Spielberg inside, ordering extra potato skins. What do you shout?*

a. "Where's Susan Sontag when you really need her?"

b. "Hello. Do you understand the meaning of potato skins beyond the Crab Nebula?"

c. "Clear the area! I just had an immaculate misconception!"

d. "Steve, babe, have I got a script for you... these aliens land behind a Wendy's at a shopping mall and..."

10 *Right in the middle of "the act", you have an image of Ann Landers mud-wrestling with Dr. Ruth Westheimer. To eliminate this thought you:*

a. Imagine the referee is Liberace.

b. Realize it's okay—you're Dolby encoded.

c. Get up and puree a pound of lamb chunks and a half dozen kiwis.

c. Apply for membership in a celibate order of Tibetan Palace Guards.

11 *You know you're having fun when:*

a. The condenser coil from your frost-free freezer emits a high, piercing squeal.

b. You can't remember anything about the Dewey Decimal System.

c. You're not wearing a tight three-piece suit made of thick, scratchy wool.

d. You just beat Jean-Paul Sartre at miniature golf.

12 *You're alone in a singles bar when a guy in a polka-dot suit comes up and says, "I'm mentally overdrawn!" You:*

a. Watch for sympathetic body language and good grooming.

b. Say, "I'm demographically corrected!"

c. Convert immediately to the Lutheran faith.

d. Grab a Devil Dog and call a few dozen toll-free numbers.

1? *You're alone in a singles bar when this ravishing creature in a polka-dot muu-muu approaches you. Trembling with desire, you:*

a. Advocate a strong national defense.

b. Say, "Here's my phone number, when you're ready for marriage give me a ring."

c. Demand a lead-lined boudoir.

d. Admit you're a chemically dependent sitcom co-star.

14 *Read the statements below and answer A for agree, D for disagree:*

a. "In a Dirtball home, the refrigerator is used primarily for display and personal expression purposes."

b. "Laundry is the fifth dimension."

c. "All life is a blur of Republicans and meat."

d. "You can buy everything you need to build a working nuclear device from a Frederick's of Hollywood catalog."

15 *True or False:*

a. Frivolity is a stern taskmaster.

b. Zombies rule Belgium.

c. Life is an endless parade of transsexual quilting bees.

d. Eddie Haskell founded Scientology.

16 *Fun is:*

a. Two rocks.

b. Four logs.

c. Three rocks.

d. Eight sardines.

17 *Julia Child and your Uncle Murray show up unannounced for brunch. You panic, then realize you have everything necessary for a gourmet feast. You serve:*

a. Froot Loops and mayo with licorice whips on a seven-grain bun.

b. A fresh roulade of wonton wrappers and wintergreen mints with a frosty mug of lime and clam juice.

c. A tureen of uncooked cream of mushroom soup blended with D-Zerta butterscotch mix and ouzo, garnished with bran buds.

d. All of the above.

18 *You're enjoying small talk at an intimate cocktail party with an attractive orthodontist. Suddenly, you realize she's an alien being because:*

a. Her ears protrude from her hair.

b. She knows too much about modems, graphic equalizers and cruise control.

c. Her Norma Kamali boatneck jersey is made in Korea.

d. She asks for more clam dip.

19 *On a vacation in Peking you notice the local "Sizzler" has a special on "twice cooked bratwurst". Inside, patrons do the mambo to a Moroccan bluegrass band. Posters of Whoopi Goldberg are everywhere. You reach for the marinated squid bits and bump your head violently on the sneeze guard. Rod Serling escorts you to a booth but his thick Japanese accent makes comprehension impossible. The thirty inch bell bottoms you're wearing are:*

a. 65% polyester, 35% cotton.

b. Nylon tricot bonded to 100% acrylic.

c. Orlon velour.

d. Wanted for armed robbery in twelve states.

HOW TO SCORE YOUR ANSWERS

1.	a. 1	b. 3	c. 2	d. 4	
2.	a. 3	b. 1	c. 2	d. 4	
3.	(E)	(S)	(F)	(U)	
a.	2	4	3	1	
b.	5	2	1	2	
c.	4	3	2	1	
d.	1	3	4	2	
e.	1	3	2	4	
4.	a. 2	b. 1	c. 4	d. 3	
5.	a. 1	b. 2	c. 1	d. 2	e. 2
6.	a. 2	b. 1	c. 1	d. 4	e. 2
7.	a. 4	b. 1	c. 2	d. 3	
8.	a. 3	b. 2	c. 4	d. 1	
9.	a. 2	b. 1	c. 4	d. 3	
10.	a. 1	b. 4	c. 3	d. 2	
11.	a. 3	b. 2	c. 1	d. 4	
12.	a. 1	b. 3	c. 2	d. 4	
13.	a. 2	b. 1	c. 4	d. 3	
14.	(A)	(D)			
a.	4	1			
b.	5	0			
c.	5	0			
d.	3	2			
15.	(T)	(F)			
a.	3	2			
b.	3	2			
c.	2	3			
d.	4	1			
16.	a. 0	b. 0	c. 10	d. 0	
17.	a. 2	b. 1	c. 1	d. 6	
18.	a. 1	b. 2	c. 3	d. 4	
19.	a. 2	b. 2	c. 3	d. 5	

RANDOM ACTIVITIES 29

YOUR FUN QUOTIENT

HERE'S WHAT YOUR SCORE MEANS

97 to 124

YOU ARE HAVING FUN YOU REALIZE THAT FUN IS A STATE OF MIND (AND TAKES SIX **TRIPLE-A BATTERIES.**)... ALSO, YOU ARE TOTALLY SAFETY-SEALED !!

65 to 96

YOU WILL SOON BE HAVING FUN
FUN IS JUST AROUND THE **CORNER** !! NOW WALK UP THREE FLIGHTS, TAKE A **NUMBER**, SIT DOWN & IT'LL BE RIGHT WITH YOU.

64 or less

YOU NEED FURTHER FUN COUNSELING
NO NEED TO WORRY, **PROFESSIONAL HELP** IS AVAILABLE.. SESSIONS ARE CONFIDENTIAL.. AMAZING RESULTS HAVE BEEN ACHIEVED.

Good Night ZIPPy

HE'S **ASLEEP**... GUESS HE FINALLY RAN OUT OF NON-SEQUITURS..

FUN IS NEVER HAVING TO SAY YOU'RE **SUSHI** !!

The author takes full responsibility for his pinhead's actions and has, off and on, since 1970. In 1986, *Zippy* celebrates ten years in weekly syndication as well as numerous appearances in magazines, paperbacks and merchandise catalogs, both domestic and foreign. This is a long time to have been so consistently inconsistent and still find time for wind-surfing and sushi.